IMAGES
*of America*

# LOST ATTRACTIONS
# OF SEVIER COUNTY

This pre-1970 aerial view of Gatlinburg's main strip includes several then-prominent businesses that today qualify as "lost attractions," among them: (1) the Mountain View Hotel, (2) Brass Lantern Restaurant, (3) Cliff Dwellers craft shop, (4) Rebel Corner, (5) Parkway Restaurant, (6) Lazy Susan Restaurant, (7) Smokyland Motel, (8) Hotel Greystone, (9) Howard Johnson's, and (10) Homespun Valley Mountaineer Village. This book will pay visits to many of these spots. (Tim Hollis collection.)

ON THE COVER: Goldrush Junction is one of the most fondly remembered attractions in the Great Smoky Mountains. The Western-themed park featured a train ride on the Goldrush, Pigeon Forge, Gatlinburg and Western (GPFG&W) railroad through many synthetic dangers, requiring a new group of young deputies to be sworn in by the marshal before each trip. (Tim Hollis collection.)

IMAGES
*of America*

# LOST ATTRACTIONS
# OF SEVIER COUNTY

Tim Hollis and
Mitzi Soward

ARCADIA
PUBLISHING

Published by Arcadia Publishing
Charleston, South Carolina

Library of Congress Control Number: 2011920542

For all general information, please contact Arcadia Publishing:
Telephone 843-853-2070
Fax 843-853-0044
E-mail sales@arcadiapublishing.com
For customer service and orders:
Toll-Free 1-888-313-2665

Visit us on the Internet at www.arcadiapublishing.com

This sort of view of Pigeon Forge is a lost attraction all its own. Mitzi Foster and her mother posed with the family car at the entrance to the Rebel Railroad (with a driving range and Rock City barn in the background) in 1962. (Mitzi Soward collection.)

# CONTENTS

# ACKNOWLEDGMENTS

Although both of the authors of this book have accumulated memorabilia relating to the tourism history of Sevier County—some of it preserved on purpose, some of it accidentally—they still found themselves canvassing family and acquaintances to fill in the holes in the story. Mitzi Soward wishes to thank Shelia Atchley, Pam Brannon, Ruth Cogdill, Wayne Dalton, Tim Johnson, Jerry Loveday, Carroll McMahan, and Anita May Maples for answering her earnest calls for help.

Tim Hollis gathered much more material than he could use when working on his exhaustive history of the area's tourism past, *The Land of the Smokies* (University Press of Mississippi, 2007), and much of the overflow has found its way into this volume. For their help with both the original book and this one, he would tip his hat—if he wore one—to Rod Bennett, Becky Craddock, Kirk Demarais, Cliff Holman, Bob Howard, Loren "Yogi" Jones, Pat Morrison, Warren Reed, Debra Jane Seltzer, Jim Sidwell Jr., Judy Ward, and Cyndy Woller.

# INTRODUCTION

At this point, you may be asking, "Just what *is* a 'lost attraction,' anyway?" Well, in the context of this book, the term has a rather broad definition, but there are at least some parameters.

At its most basic, when we say "lost attractions," we can mean any sort of tourist-oriented business that no longer exists. For most people, that conjures up images of true roadside attractions: Pigeon Forge's Fairyland or Magic World, for example, or Gatlinburg's Jolly Golf or Tour Through Hell. Since tourists have to subsist on amenities as well as sightseeing, though, we have also chosen to include such other establishments as motels, restaurants, and an occasional souvenir store or service station.

If you casually flip through these pages, you might find yourself putting on the brakes and saying, "Wait! That place is still in business!" And, in some cases, you might be right. We still classify it as a "lost attraction" if its present-day appearance varies greatly from its origins—for example, today's Ripley's *Believe It Or Not!* Museum bears scant resemblance to its original 1968 building. Likewise, Pigeon Forge still has a miniature golf course known as Fantasy Golf, but it looks nothing like the mid-1980s photograph you will see here.

In an area with a long history of tourism such as Sevier County, it is inevitable that older attractions would have to give way for new ones. If all the attractions, motels, and restaurants depicted in this book were still in business, combined with all the ones that have come along since, the US 441 corridor would be even more congested than it already is. Whenever possible, we have tried to put this ever-changing face in perspective by noting the evolution of certain hot spots: the legendary Fort Weare Game Park, for instance, later became the site of Magic World, which is today the site of Professor Hacker's Lost Treasure Golf. The property formerly occupied by the fabled Fairyland became home to a Ponderosa Steakhouse, and as of this writing sits as a weed-infested vacant lot. How many tourists today stop to realize that Pigeon Forge's showplace, Dollywood, still shows evidence of its earlier lives as Silver Dollar City, Goldrush Junction, and the Rebel Railroad?

With such a vast array of material, both in our own collections and generously loaned to us by the individuals credited on each, one of the first steps was to come up with a way to arrange it all. The first chapter and the last chapter are somewhat funhouse mirror reflections of each other: chapter one contains attractions and businesses that were uniquely suited to their Great Smoky Mountains locale, many of them themed around the area's two most common images, bears and hillbillies. By contrast, the final chapter is devoted to tourist spots that did not seem to fit into their surroundings. Many of them had such short lives that they are remembered only for the postcards and other fading ephemera they left behind. In between, individual chapters are devoted wholly to defunct restaurants, celebrity-driven attractions, dinosaurs and other fantastic sights, and of course, the story of the theme park known variously as the Rebel Railroad, Goldrush Junction, and Silver Dollar City. If you do not know what became of that place, you certainly haven't been in Sevier County for very long.

Speaking of that, it is probably appropriate to point out that the two authors of this book have vastly different personal experiences with Sevier County. Hopefully having two perspectives will help convey the whole story more than either could have done alone. Mitzi Soward has lived in the Tennessee hills all her life, originally in Knoxville and then, beginning in 1965, in Sevierville. Her father owned the Bears' Den Motel on the busy US 441 strip, so the family was able to observe the region's growing and changing tourism business firsthand.

On the other side of the coin, Tim Hollis lives near Birmingham, Alabama, and his experience with the Smokies was much as Mitzi's family and the other business owners wanted: as a tourist. Beginning in 1966, when he was three years old, Hollis and his elders made semi-regular pilgrimages to Gatlinburg and Pigeon Forge to sample the ever-evolving attractions available.

These two different views on the subject mean that some of the places represented in this book were more important from a local standpoint, while others were almost ignored by Sevier County residents and appealed only to those out-of-towners who ventured into the neighborhood. It is the wish of both authors that, as you read through the pages that follow, you will not necessarily be aware of who wrote which captions—although occasionally there may be tattletale clues if you look closely enough.

So, that should be enough introduction. Some of you are probably already impatiently flipping through pages, looking for something you remember, and far be it from us to stop you. Let's hit the highway together and visit the Gatlinburg, Pigeon Forge, and Sevierville that used to be.

—Tim Hollis and Mitzi Soward

Tim Hollis (with his hands keeping the sun out of his face) visited the Smokies with his family for the first time in August 1966. Here they are stopping for lunch at Gatlinburg's now-departed Howard Johnson's restaurant. (Tim Hollis collection.)

# One

# HOME IN THE HILLS

No single element could be more emblematic of the Smokies than the region's black bears. Reports are that the Smoky Cub Motor Court was originally known as the Smoky Bear, but the US Forest Service thought that name was a little too close to its own trademarked character. (Mitzi Soward collection.)

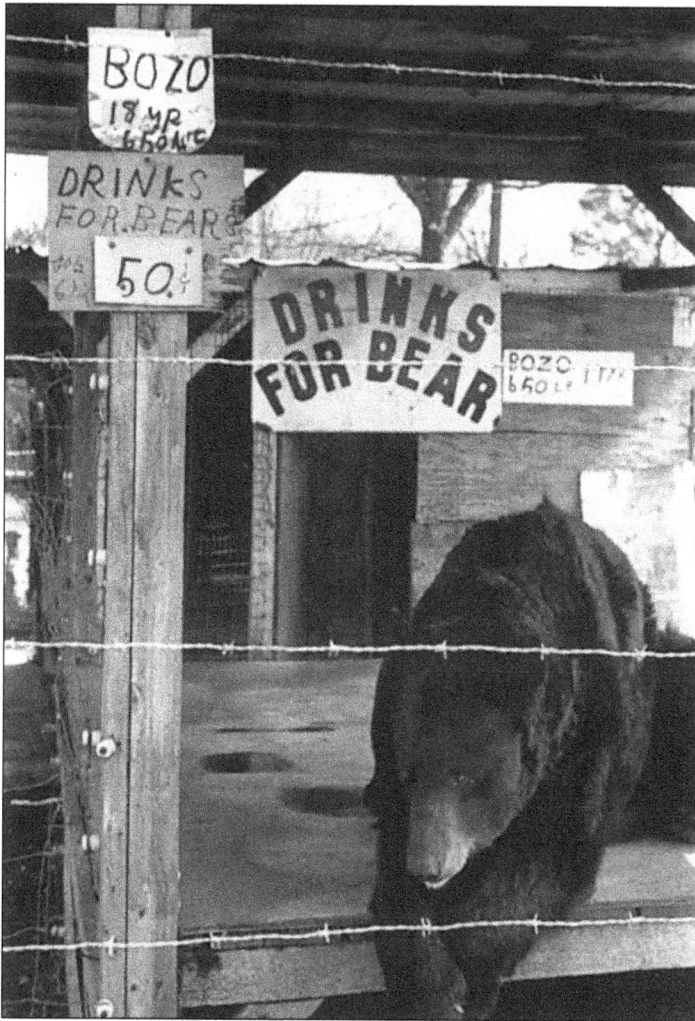

Bozo was one bear that visitors to the Smokies were sure to see on their pilgrimage to the mountains. Located alongside the main highway leading to the Great Smoky Mountains National Park, he was more accessible than the bears tourists hoped to spy in their natural habitat. He also had an unusual craving for chocolate milk, which his owners would sell to tourists to give him. This sort of captivity is rightfully frowned upon today, and Bozo's expression bears out the reasons why. (Carroll McMahan collection.)

Besides roadside attractions, motels also used the appealing bears to get travelers to stop and hibernate a while. The Bearskin Motel used this "dancing bears" photograph in its advertising long after the two subject bruins had likely gone to their happy hunting grounds. (Tim Hollis collection.)

Not all roadside bears were the realistic type. California-based TraveLodge had been employing "Sleepy Bear" as its mascot for years, but the drowsy logo never looked as much at home as in Gatlinburg. (Tim Hollis collection.)

Kampy the Bear, logo character for Kamp-Rite Acres, bore more than a passing resemblance to that more famous pic-a-nic basket thief, Yogi Bear. (Tim Hollis collection.)

11

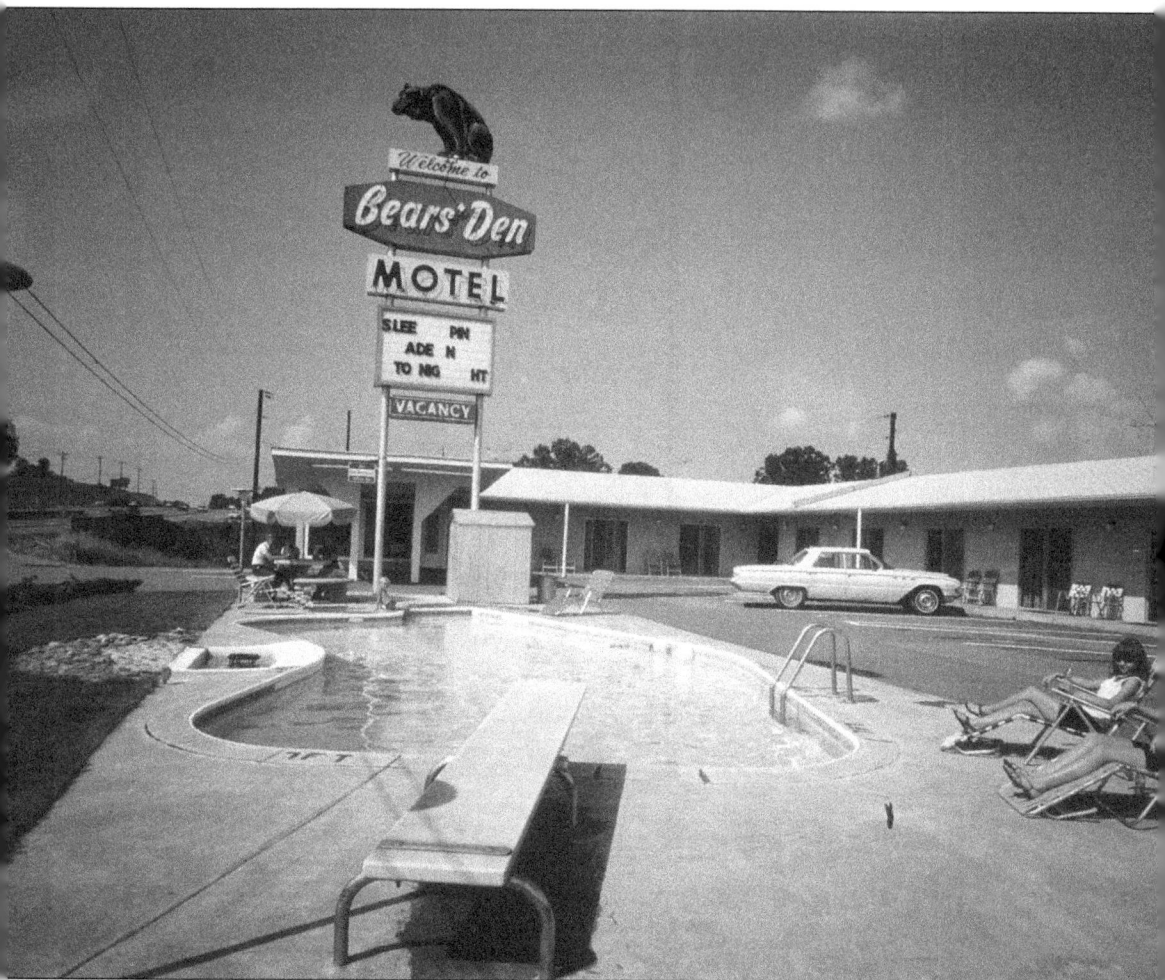

Using the slogan, "Sleep in a Den Tonight," the Bears' Den Motel was one of many mom-and-pop establishments alongside Highway 441 that offered lodging for tourists. With a season lasting from Memorial Day through October, this establishment took its cue from the bears and hibernated during the rest of the year. It opened in 1965 and was run by Bill and Charlotte Foster until late 1971, when it changed hands. Ultimately, it was razed in the name of progress, and a patch of grass is all that remains to mark a portion of its site. (Tim Hollis collection.)

Closely trailing the bears in popularity were hillbillies. Even though the locals were generally not thrilled with the image, they were not opposed to employing it for their advertising, as with these Bear's Den Motel matchbooks. (Mitzi Soward collection.)

After all these years, no one seems to remember where in Pigeon Forge the Hillbilly Museum was located, or what sort of displays it contained. It is truly a lost attraction—lost even from residents' minds. (Tim Hollis collection.)

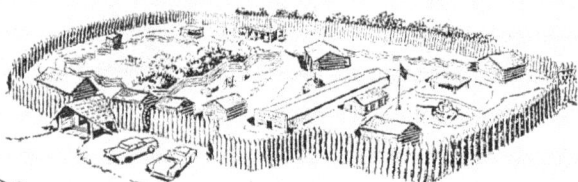

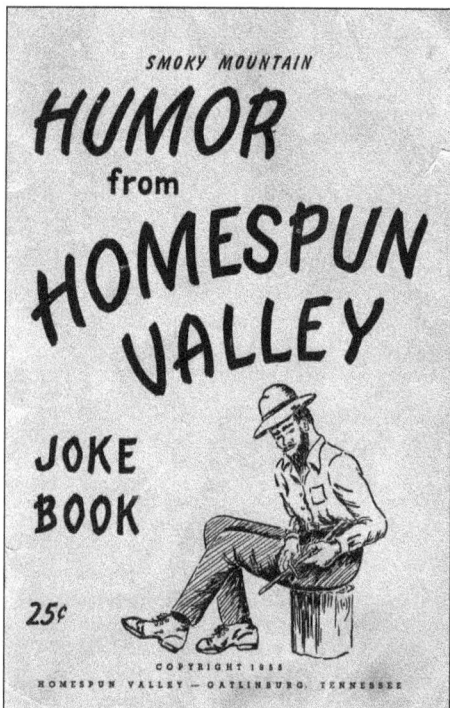

Since the 1920s, Gatlinburg had been known primarily as a collection of handicraft shops. In 1951, Homespun Valley Mountaineer Village opened as what might well be termed the first true tourist attraction in town. (Tim Hollis collection.)

Homespun Valley endeavored to present pioneer life as it really existed in the Smokies, but it frequently lapsed into standard hillbilly humor, just as with so many of its roadside companions. (Cyndy Woller collection.)

# You'll Have Family Fun —

Native mountaineers "makin' mountain music" every night

Every member of the family will enjoy it.

Demonstrating the old time treadle lathe

# Living The Life Of A Pioneer, At —

Grinding corn meal the old-fashioned way.

The Pink Huskey mountaineer cabin

Boring a hog rifle by hand

# Homespun Valley Mountaineer Village

A mountaineer's log barn and farm tools

Barn dancing every Saturday night

A corner of an authentic mountain cabin

# An Unforgettable Experience —

Selling stone-ground corn meal at the store

A corner of the old-time country store

The Village blacksmith turns a shoe

This incredible foldout spread from one of Homespun Valley's brochures of the 1950s gives us a dozen-for-one view of some of its attractions. Homespun Valley was spun home in the mid-1970s, and its former site on Airport Road is now part of the parking lot for Gatlinburg's Civic Center. (Tim Hollis collection.)

LARGEST STILL EVER CAPTURED IN TENN.
This 1500 Gallon Still Was Found In The Loft Of
Large Dairy Barn In Knox County In May 1962.
It Was Fired With Gas To Eliminate Smoke.
Captured With This STILL Was 432 Bags Of Sugar.
10 Barrels Of Pure Corn Mash And 119 Gallons Of
120 Proof MOONSHINE Whiskey.
This Story Is True, But The Names Are Not
Mentioned To Protect The GUILTY.

One hillbilly attraction that has not been lost in Pigeon Forge's changing tourist landscape is Hill-Billy Village. However, even though some of these same displays can still be seen, the plywood cartoon mountaineers pictured in these postcards have long since made their final moonshine run. (Tim Hollis collection.)

MOONSHINE STILL

The Ogle family has been prominent in Sevier County tourism for decades. As you can see, they too went the comical hillbilly route for their motel advertising. (Tim Hollis collection.)

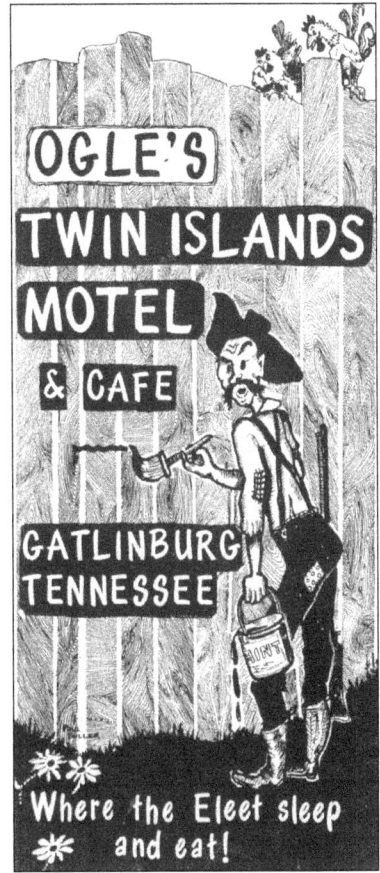

OGLE'S
TWIN ISLANDS
MOTEL
& CAFE

GATLINBURG
TENNESSEE

Where the Eleet sleep and eat!

This pottery and gift shop on US Highway 441, north of Sevierville, used its own renditions of Fred Lasswell's *Barney Google and Snuffy Smith* comic strip cast to decorate its signage and exterior walls. (Tim Hollis collection.)

LAST CHANCE
DINNERWARE

POTTERY
Closeout

Gatlinburg's lodging industry began with Andrew Huff's Mountain View Hotel in 1916. It stood for many years at the crossroads where weary travelers approached the city from the north and east. (Jerry Loveday collection.)

Enjoy the GREAT SMOKY MOUNTAINS NATIONAL PARK from the

**Mountain View** HOTEL and MOTOR LODGE

GATLINBURG, TENNESSEE

*The Nationally Renowned*
**HOTEL DINING ROOM**

*Your*
**VACATION WONDERLAND**

Our home-cooked Southern food is served in our traditional family style. Among the most appealing dishes are country ham, fried chicken, hot biscuits, honey & jam. A la Carte selections also available. Dining room attire is informal and the general public is welcome.

Golfing enthusiasts can have the pleasure of playing on the Gatlinburg Country Club course. This $250,000 course presents scenic vistas and panoramas at every green and tee.

Your *Master Hosts* in Gatlinburg

Although the Mountain View was eventually replaced by other ventures, the Huff family's hospitality is still alive in various other businesses around Gatlinburg. The hotel was beloved by many east Tennesseans as well as visitors from afar. (Tim Hollis collection.)

The Smoky Mt. Plaza Motel was opened by Lee and Verla Crosno in 1952. Its unusual (for the mountains) aqua-and-pink color scheme was Vera's favorite combination, and also stemmed from the couple's original intent to open a motel on one of the Florida beaches. On their way back from scouting locations in the Sunshine State, they stopped off in Gatlinburg and decided that they liked that spot even better. The motel maintained its funky architecture and color palette until it closed shortly after Lee's death in 1974. (Tim Hollis collection.)

A brand new Howard Johnson's Motor Lodge at Gatlinburg, Tenn.

A brand new Howard Johnson's Motor Lodge is now open in the heart of Gatlinburg.

The soundproof rooms feature specially designed sleeping, dressing and bathing areas and both indoor and outdoor patio living areas for your comfort and relaxation.

Through the use of connecting doorways, a variety of various combinations of rooms are available to offer the perfect room arrangement for a single traveler or for an entire family on vacation.

There's a modern swimming pool and wide spacious grounds. There's even a Howard Johnson's Restaurant adjacent to the Motor Lodge for your dining convenience. All of this is available at Howard Johnson's sensible prices.

● TEXACO—AMER. EXPRESS—CARTE BLANCHE—DINERS' CLUB ●

# HOWARD JOHNSON'S
## "Host of the Highways"

One of the first chain motels to enter the Smokies was Howard Johnson's, previously best known for its restaurants. Its orange roof's arrival in the early 1960s was soon followed by Holiday Inn, Best Western, and all the others. (Tim Hollis collection)

The Bilmar Motor Inn in Pigeon Forge is now known as the Quality Inn and Suites. Look closely at the background, and it's clear that the Bilmar sat directly opposite the entrance to the Goldrush Junction theme park. (Tim Hollis collection.)

Glenn Glass was a former football player for the University of Tennessee and, later, in the NFL. When he got into the tourism business with the Smokyland Motel, he was not shy about using his name recognition. (Tim Hollis collection.)

Another ex-football player who made it big in the Smokies' tourism industry was Charles "Z" Buda. His business ventures ranged from motels to restaurants and attractions. His campground in Pigeon Forge lasted long enough to have its own web site, but it is now padlocked and abandoned. (Tim Hollis collection.)

Colorful • Exquisite • Inspiring
(NON-DENOMINATIONAL)

At Christus Biblical Gardens you see and
hear unfolded in rare beauty the
"Greatest Story Ever Told," presented in the
world's foremost depiction of the life
of Christ by lifelike Biblical characters
dramatically staged in realistic
Holy Land scenes.

On the River Road
GATLINBURG, TENNESSEE
"in the Smokies"

While Ronald S. Ligon was a sophomore at Vanderbilt University, he contracted a severe case of tuberculosis. He promised God that if he came through his illness, he would build some sort of significant memorial to divine providence. (Tim Hollis collection.)

GATLINBURG'S
Christus
Biblical
Gardens

MAJOR ALL-YEAR
VISITOR ATTRACTION
IN THE SMOKIES

ON RIVER ROAD
NEXT TO THE SKY LIFT

NON-DENOMINATIONAL

Ligon indeed recovered from his tuberculosis bout, and making good on his promise, opened Christus Biblical Gardens in Gatlinburg on August 13, 1960. (Tim Hollis collection.)

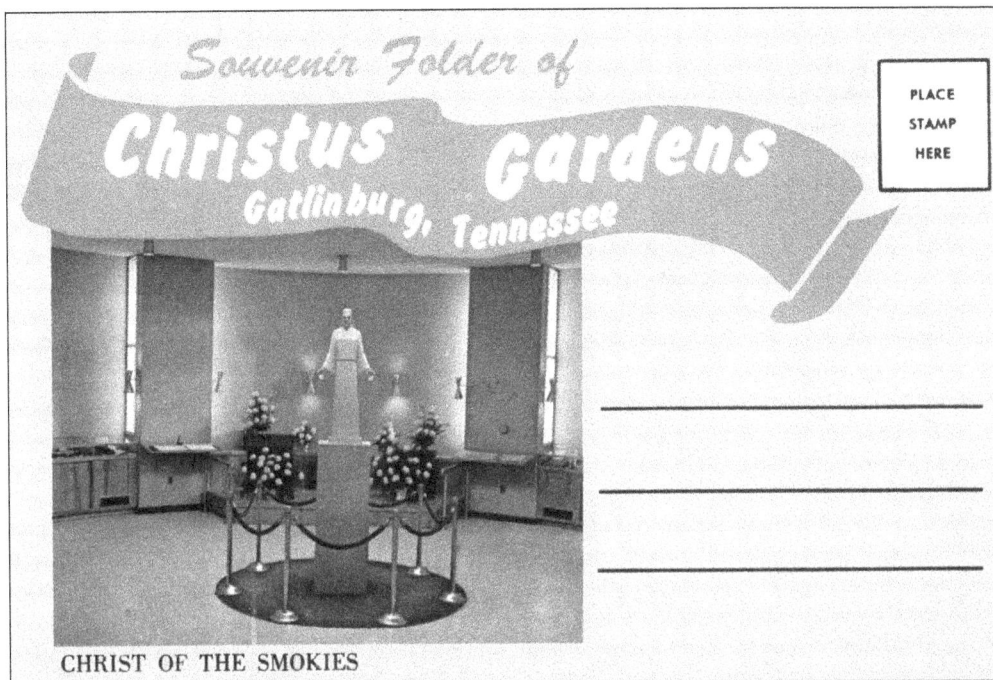

CHRIST OF THE SMOKIES

At Christus Gardens (as the name was eventually shortened), the life of Christ was played out in a series of wax dioramas. This statue in the rotunda was the "Christus" from which the attraction took its name. (Tim Hollis collection.)

One of the most photographed displays at Christus Gardens was this marble face of Christ. As this montage from one of the brochures shows, it was carved in such a way as to follow the viewer in any direction. (Tim Hollis collection.)

23

It was only natural that the Nativity scene would be the first one visitors encountered in Christus Gardens' galleries. For many years, there was no baby Jesus in the tableau, only a glow coming from the manger. (Tim Hollis collection.)

In this scene, Satan appears to be telling Jesus, "Over there would be a wonderful spot to build a condominium." Someone else must have been listening to Beelzebub, because in 2008, Christus Gardens closed so that it could be demolished for just such a venture. (Tim Hollis collection.)

Miraculously, Christus Gardens enjoyed its own resurrection of sorts. The condominium idea fell through, and even though the original 1960 wax scenes had been sold, a group of former employees reopened the attraction as the Christ in the Smokies Museum, with all-new figures depicting the same views as the originals. (Tim Hollis collection.)

# NATIONAL BIBLE MUSEUM®

## GATLINBURG, TENNESSEE

### RIVER OAKS CENTER
River Road

### SEE

HUNDREDS OF BIBLES
IN SCORES OF
LANGUAGES
FROM ALL OVER
THE WORLD

**FIRST EDITION COPIES**

Eastern America's
**MOST UNUSUAL COLLECTION**

Other Christian-themed attractions made a pilgrimage to the Smokies to bask in Christus Gardens' reflected glory. The National Bible Museum was not one of the more memorable of these, but in Chapter Six are some others that took the concept in a completely different direction. (Tim Hollis collection.)

Aunt Mahalia's candy stores can still be found in several Gatlinburg locations, but it has been many years since they sported the gingerbread cottage look of this, the original location, as seen in a 1956 postcard. Aunt Mahalia's is said to date back to 1939, making it the oldest candy shop in Gatlinburg, and the grandmother (or aunt) of the many, many others that would follow. (Cyndy Woller collection.)

The 1950s were indubitably a simpler time in mountain tourism, and even seemingly insignificant businesses such as a Shell service station issued their own postcards. Notice that the building employed the "mountain stone" look that was extremely popular for roadside architecture in the region. (Bob Howard collection.)

Another classic 1950s Gatlinburg service station was this Phillips 66 outlet, with its distinctive highway shield–shaped glass globes topping the pumps. To discover why a miniature train is gassing up here, rather than an automobile, turn to page 77. (Loren "Yogi" Jones collection.)

THESE ARE THE
CANDLES YOU HEAR
SO MUCH ABOUT

*Candelier*
Reg. U. S. Pat. Office

**Candlemaking**

**Candles**

Like You Never Saw Before!

Guaranteed heat - proof
and travel - safe

We are dedicated
to original design,
unique color and the
quality of fine craftsmanship

( LOOK FOR·
THIS SIGN )

ON U. S. 441
915 PARKWAY

Across from City Parking
Lot Nearest to Entrance
to Great Smoky Mountains
National Park

Come visit with us

WATCH US WORK - - -
Chat-a-bit and enjoy an
adventure into the
candle world.

Some craft shops in Gatlinburg have remained in business for decades, but one of the casualties was the Candelier store. It was as noted for its giant candle signage as for its handcrafted wax candles. (Tim Hollis collection.)

This 1953 linen postcard scene is one of the most common views of Gatlinburg's main drag as it appeared then. On the left side of the street is the Edgepark Motel, and on the right is the original Cliff Dwellers Shop, one of Gatlinburg's earliest and most durable craft stores. (Jerry Loveday collection.)

More of Gatlinburg's emerging character can be discerned from these two different street views, the one above from 1959 and the one below from 1967. Among the visible businesses are the Park Tourist Court and Bill's Restaurant—in its own stone-surfaced building—as well as the sign for Don Ward's crafts and antiques store, which partially obscures the original style flashing-lights crown of the Best Western motel. (Loren "Yogi" Jones collection.)

This 1958 advertisement is one of the earliest images of the Rebel Corner, a huge souvenir shop that sat at the busy intersection of US 441 and Airport Road in Gatlinburg. (Tim Hollis collection.)

By the 1970s, the Rebel Corner had grown to two stories and was a sight no tourist could miss. However, it never even had the chance to be doomed by political correctness. It was destroyed by a 1992 fire that began with a faulty lighted sign in the T-shirt shop next door; the fire also consumed the adjoining Ripley's *Believe It or Not!* Museum. (Warren Reed collection.)

Ogle's Water Park was one of the most popular summertime destinations for locals and visitors alike. With its wave pool, exciting water slides, giant "kiddie" pool, and various concession stands, it was practically an amusement park for landlocked beach lovers. Visitors were able to have the best of both worlds in the Smokies. (Tim Hollis collection.)

Hey Mama -- What's A "Rama"?
See
**Cherokee-RAMA**
GATLINBURG'S "TRAIL OF TEARS"

See exciting siege of Fort Loudoun

See Battle of Horseshoe Bend

See villages attacked

**THE CHEROKEE INDIAN STORY**

See the tragic "Trail of Tears"

Generally speaking, the story of the area's Native Americans was the theme of Cherokee, North Carolina, on the other side of the Smokies from Sevier County. However, in the 1960s, Gatlinburg got its own Cherokee-themed attraction, created by the same team that operated the very similar Confederama at the base of Lookout Mountain in Chattanooga. Apparently by the time of this brochure, the 1950s craze for adding "-rama" to the end of attraction names was already growing stale, prompting a slogan that made fun of its own moniker. (Tim Hollis collection.)

In the early 1980s, two out-of-their-element attractions tried to find a niche in Gatlinburg. Family Showstreet USA tried to be everything to everyone, including a clone of Disney's Country Bear Jamboree and a Theatre of the Stars that could not decide whether it was saluting Elvis Presley or John Lennon. (Tim Hollis collection.)

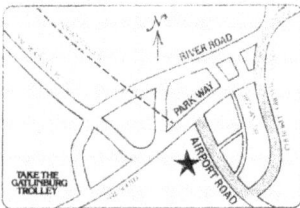

Gatlinburg Place took an even more scattershot approach to entertainment than Family Showstreet USA, but it ventured even closer to Disney trademark territory with its Backwoods Bear Jamboree. The park did not survive for long, and today, only a few of its former buildings—repurposed for other usage—serve to indicate that it ever existed at all. (Tim Hollis collection.)

# Two

# WHAT'S FOR
# VITTLES, GRANNY?

Even before chains such as Cracker Barrel brought "down-home cooking" to a national audience, the Smokies had plenty of restaurants that fit the same mold. Granny's in Sevierville even looked a lot like the later Cracker Barrel building style, with the addition of a cartoon grandma to serve as a logo. (Tim Hollis collection.)

Even though it had no particular theme that fit into its Smokies home, Gatlinburg's Parkway Restaurant made up for that with longevity. Here are two different eras' versions of the same building. The photograph above dates from the 1950s and shows the tall, vertical neon sign, while the lower photograph is from the early 1970s. The shape of the original building was still discernable after 20 years of remodeling. (Tim Hollis collection.)

Their legendary appetites made bears as valuable for restaurants as they were for motels and gift shops. This particular view of the Big Bear Restaurant in Pigeon Forge also reminds us of the now-forgotten Red Carpet Inns motel chain. (Tim Hollis collection.)

The Black Bear Restaurant on US 321 in Gatlinburg used a more realistic bear on its signage, rather than a cartoon character. Like several other businesses, this version of the Black Bear was later blacked out by a fire. (Tim Hollis collection.)

If bears were in the restaurant business, could hillbillies be far behind? This souvenir placemat from Hobie's Copper Still in Gatlinburg left unanswered the question of whether the overall-clad gun-totin' hillbilly was male or female. (Tim Hollis collection.)

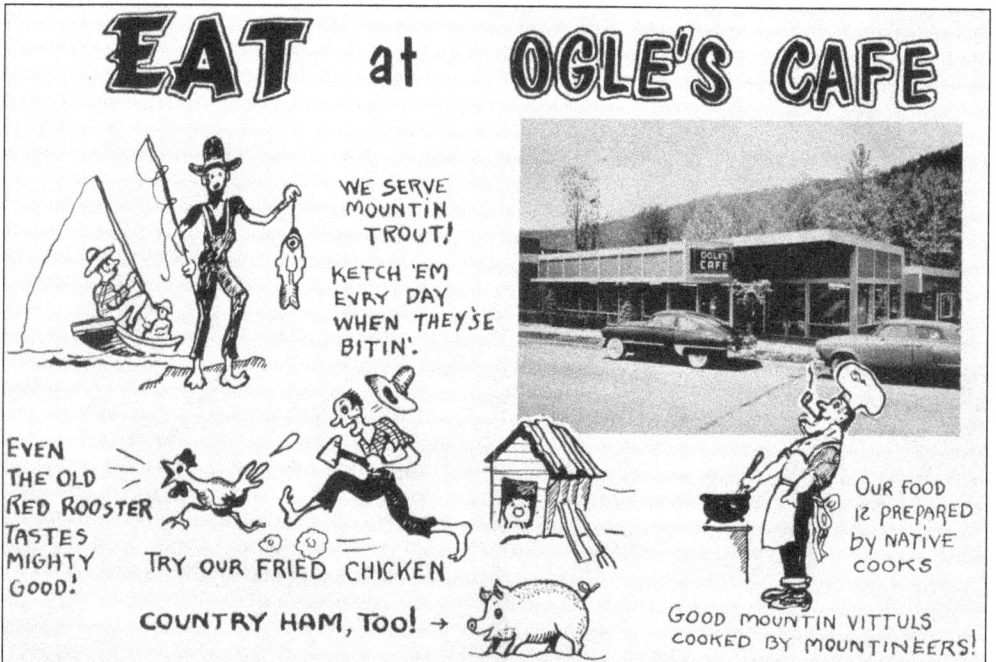

Ogle's Café left no doubt as to its geographical location by throwing cartoon hillbillies and comical dialect into its advertising. Tourists definitely knew they were not in Brooklyn. (Tim Hollis collection.)

The Little Brown Jug Restaurant in Gatlinburg looked modern on the outside, but the neon sign stayed close to its roots with its depiction of a jug of potent white lightnin'. (Jerry Loveday collection.)

The red-and-white stripes on the roof were not fooling anyone: the Gateway Restaurant in Pigeon Forge was obviously housed in a building that formerly contained one of the Horne's candy stores. When Horne's moved out, they left their crown logo on the front as a telltale remnant. (Tim Hollis collection.)

Decked out in crisp classy uniforms, the staff at the Open Hearth Restaurant welcomed hungry tourists looking for a more upscale dining experience. The establishment specialized in steaks cooked to perfection. While many business owners favored the region's black bears or hillbillies in order to get the attention of passersby, the Open Hearth chose a theme in line with its product. However, things could not get too stuffy as long as the Open Hearth had that giant bull on top of its sign. (Tim Hollis collection.)

Earlier, we mentioned Z Buda as one of Pigeon Forge's tourism tycoons. One of his many business ventures was Bunting's Apple Tree Inn, a restaurant that featured outdoor dining with a spectacular view of the mountains to increase one's appetite. (Jerry Loveday collection.)

**Next to the Park-Gatlinburg's Best**

burning bush
restaurant

1151 Parkway • Gatlinburg, Tennessee

As its slogan indicated, the Burning Bush Restaurant was the last business before US 441 entered the Great Smoky Mountains National Park and all commercialism ceased—until the highway emerged into Cherokee on the other side, at least. (Tim Hollis collection.)

Kentucky Fried Chicken came to Gatlinburg in the days before the chain had its own sit-down restaurant. The tasty treat was served as a menu item at other restaurants, or else offered through small carryout buildings such as this one. (Mitzi Soward collection.)

Of course, those of us over a certain age are immediately familiar with this KFC building design of the late 1960s and early 1970s, with its striped pagoda roof and Colonel Sanders weathervane. (Tim Hollis collection.)

Remac's Drive-In was for many years a popular spot for families, tourists, and young couples alike. Located near the area's only drive-in movie theater (the Midway), it was usually full of teens on the weekends. They served up "baskets" of yummy meals and ice cream either in the dining room or in the comfort of your automobile. Locals loved it, and those of us lucky enough to have dined there still miss it. (Mitzi Soward collection.)

Johnson's Drive-In was practically a chain; it had a restaurant in Sevierville as well as one in Gatlinburg. The weekends were always busy, with a constant stream of young people "circling" the Johnson's in Sevierville. (Mitzi Soward collection.)

To add to the fun, the Tastee Freez was located next door to Johnson's Drive-In, making it easy to "circle" in a figure eight, as drivers would strive to see and be seen on Friday and Saturday nights. (Mitzi Soward collection.)

Another national chain of drive-ins that drove into Sevier County was Dog 'n' Suds. Its trademark hound looked like a hybrid of Walt Disney's Pluto and Goofy. (Debra Jane Seltzer collection.)

The Lum's restaurant chain staggered into Gatlinburg with its signature menu item, hot dogs steamed in beer. Even after the chain went out of business in the early 1980s, Gatlinburg's Lum's kept operating for several more years. (Tim Hollis collection.)

Kids dine for 99¢

Kids under 12 get a choice of their three favorite meals:
- Hamburger, fries and soft drink
- Fishwich, fries and soft drink
- Hot Dog, fries and soft drink
- Plus creamy pudding and seconds on soft drinks. only 99¢

LUMS

- Sea Food
- Steaks
- Hot Dog & Burger Platters

At Lums Of Gatlinburg You Get A Lot More!

Open for Breakfast "Full Service"

You get a lot better CHOICE when you choose

LUMS

Open 8 a.m. - 1 a.m.
Airport Rd., by the Space Needle
Phone 436-7383

Lum's was something of an innovator among fast-food restaurants when it introduced a breakfast menu. Other Lum's advertisements from the late 1960s featured an endorsement from an unlikely source: Milton Berle. (Tim Hollis collection.)

After the demise of Lum's as a chain, the owners of the Gatlinburg outlet revamped the logo. Apparently they decided to connect the name "Lum's" to "lumberjack," hence the wild-eyed Paul Bunyan caricature on this 1985 menu. (Tim Hollis collection.)

Jack's Hamburgers was a fast-food chain based in Birmingham, Alabama. It opened an outpost in Gatlinburg in 1968, around the same time the company established a beachhead in Panama City Beach. (Tim Hollis collection.)

JACK'S

**OPEN FOR BUSINESS**

GATLINBURG'S NEWEST AND, MOST POPULAR EATING SPOT

HAMBURGERS

GOOD GOOD GOOD

FRENCH FRIES
PIES
SHAKES

ROAST BEEF

WE ARE LOCATED AT
CORNER RIVER ROAD & OWNBY ST.
TURN ON PARKWAY — SIGNAL 10

Nickerson Farms was a chain of restaurants/gift shops much like Stuckey's or Horne's. In 1979, what appears to have been a smaller-than-usual Nickerson Farms opened at the intersection of Interstate 40 and State Highway 66 in Kodak. (Wayne Dalton collection.)

Z Buda's ubiquitous name was attached to this pancake house, which was evidently housed in an older-style Horne's building than the Gateway Restaurant we saw back on page 39. (Tim Hollis collection.)

The Green Valley Restaurant in Pigeon Forge was located on the southernmost end of town. Along with Trotter's (home of the world's best butterscotch pie) and Bunting's Apple Tree Inn, the Green Valley saw its share of folks dressed in their Sunday best and Easter frocks as the destination of locals on those special occasions. (Tim Hollis collection.)

The Cross Ties Restaurant was an actual vintage railroad depot from Scottsboro, Alabama. It was reassembled at the entrance to Goldrush Junction. The historic building, still on the same spot, now serves as the marketing offices for Dollywood. (Tim Hollis collection.)

# *Three*

# FROM CONFEDERATE MONEY TO SILVER DOLLARS

In 1961, the Civil War centennial was getting underway. Brothers Harry and Grover Robbins, who had made an attraction out of the Tweetsie Railroad at Boone, North Carolina, opened a new park known as the Rebel Railroad in Pigeon Forge. (Tim Hollis collection.)

This photograph dates from the Rebel Railroad's earliest years. Notice that the park rounded off the number of yards required to travel the one mile from the highway to the center of action. (Mitzi Soward collection.)

When the Robbins brothers purchased an operating steam locomotive for their Rebel Railroad, they also acquired a few non-working models, such as this one, to be used for display only. (Mitzi Soward collection.)

REBEL R.R.

PIGEON FORGE, TENN.
(Near Gatlinburg, Tenn.)

As this postcard folder makes abundantly clear, in the early 1960s, the Rebel Railroad expected every one of its visitors to be totally sympathetic to the "Lost Cause" of the Confederacy. (Tim Hollis collection.)

The Robbins brothers did fudge a little when it came to the true origins of the Rebel Railroad's locomotive. Although it was unashamedly touted as "a full-size train of the Civil War era," in reality, the engine was manufactured during World War II—a rather different breed of conflict. (Tim Hollis collection.)

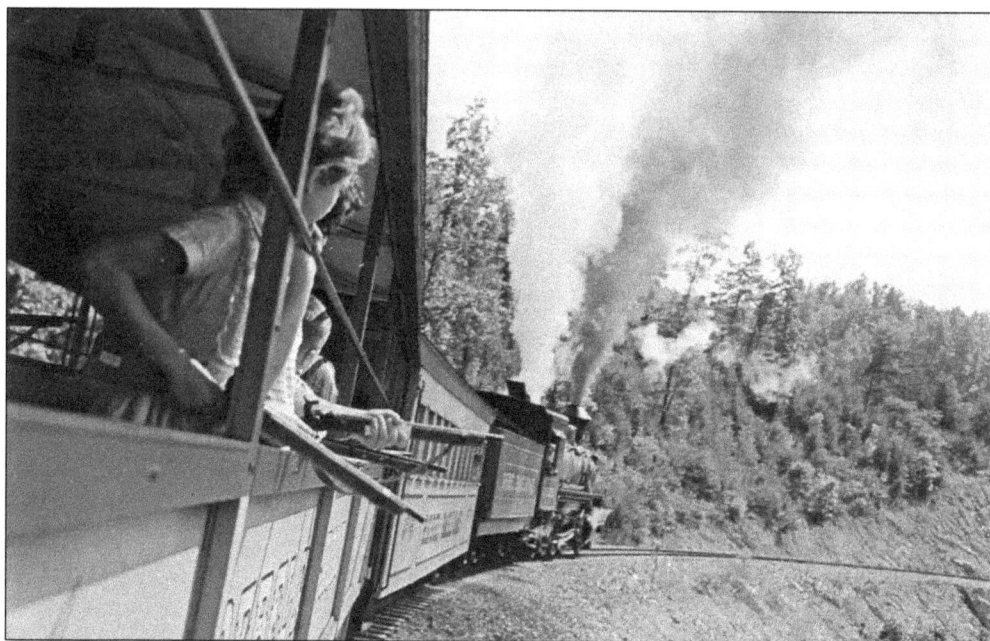

It should be obvious by now that political correctness was not a concern of the Rebel Railroad. Adding to that theme were the toy rifles handed out to the kids on the passenger list, so they could be on guard against Yankee marauders. (Tim Hollis collection.)

The high point of a trip on the Rebel Railroad was a stopover at Fort Agony, where supposedly a shipment of gold awaited transportation back to behind Confederate lines. The former site of the fort is now a huge open field. (Tim Hollis collection.)

Meanwhile, back in Rebeltown 1860, life went on at its quiet daily pace. In the early 1960s, this was the extent of the entire park, but with each new name and theme, more and more acreage would be developed. (Tim Hollis collection.)

The general store at the Rebel Railroad blended various eras of history into a single display, stocking the shelves with packaged goods that would have been commonplace in the early 1900s, but unknown in the 1860s. The general store building is the only known structure from 1961 to still exist, but even it has been remodeled beyond recognition. (Tim Hollis collection.)

Rebeltown 1860 borrowed its theme heavily from the preponderance of Western theme parks that operated around the country at the time. The Lady Gay Saloon would have been as at home in Kansas's Dodge City as it was in the Great Smoky Mountains, but all those Confederate flags left no question as to its true home region. (Tim Hollis collection.)

A real, live blacksmith plying his trade was a welcome sight throughout the Rebel Railroad, Goldrush Junction, and Silver Dollar City days. This particular blacksmith, however, bears more resemblance to W.C. Fields than to the burly village smithy of folklore. (Tim Hollis collection.)

The most common souvenir from the blacksmith shop was this horseshoe with the purchaser's name engraved into it. Examples of these still rest in forgotten boxes in attics and basements throughout Sevier County and the rest of the south. (Pat Morrison collection.)

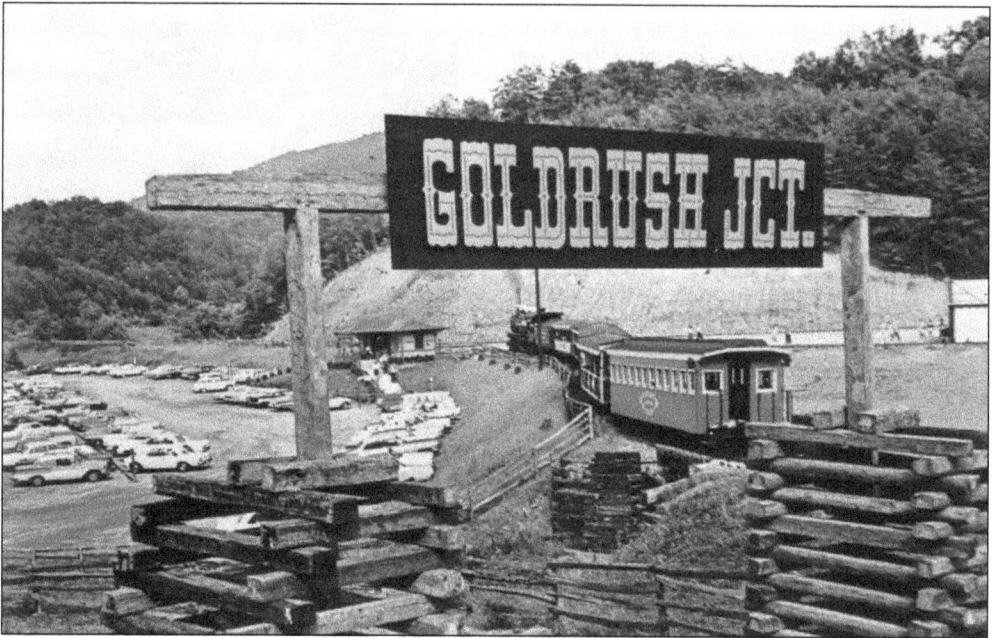

With the Civil War centennial craze beginning to die down, in 1964, the Rebel Railroad underwent minor cosmetic surgery and emerged as Goldrush Junction, evoking the era of the 1840s California Gold Rush rather than the War Between the States. At the same time, the locomotive received a new name, *Klondike Katie*, even though that evoked a different gold rush altogether. (Tim Hollis collection.)

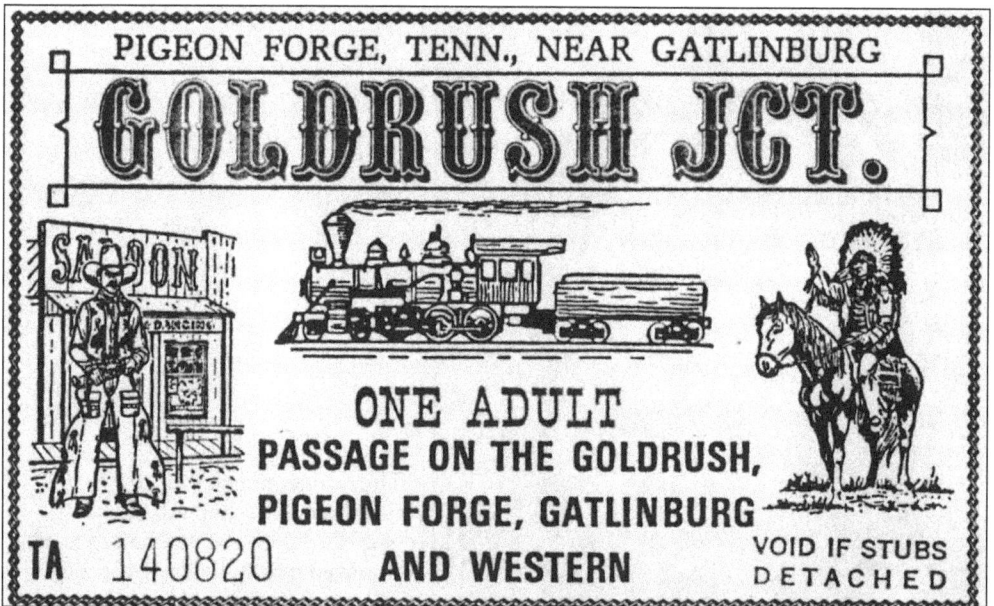

The newly-christened Goldrush, Pigeon Forge, Gatlinburg and Western (GPFG&W) railroad was still the main attraction at Goldrush Junction, but the pitfalls it encountered along the run were different. Maybe we can use this ticket to discover what they were. (Tim Hollis collection.)

Before *Klondike Katie* departed for the wilderness, the town marshal would swear in all the younger passengers as honorary deputies. In a move that might raise an eyebrow or some dander today, each new deputy was handed a toy gun to use on the bad guys. (Tim Hollis collection.)

All of the junior law enforcement officials received one of these decals to confirm their newly earned position. The fact that some kids actually preserved theirs after the trip is a good indicator of their significance. (Pat Morrison collection.)

The marshal was going to need the help of all those dinky deputies, because snakes in the weeds such as Jesse James (played here by Pat Morrison) lay in wait to steal the railroad's valuable gold shipment. (Pat Morrison collection.)

After Frank and Jesse James had purloined the gold shipment and made their getaway earlier in the trip, the marshal and his minions would find them holed up in their cabin, and justice would finally prevail. (Pat Morrison collection.)

The junior deputies would make themselves useful by helping the marshal march them thar varmints off to the hoosegow in Goldrush Junction. Somehow, they never seemed to remain captured for long, as the whole act would be repeated throughout the day. (Tim Hollis collection.)

This impressive brochure from Goldrush Junction's early years holds a secret: that trestle photograph is actually from Tweetsie Railroad. Considering that Photoshop had not yet been invented, someone did a good job of pasting the GPFG&W logo onto the photo. (Tim Hollis collection.)

Any tourist attraction worth its billboards had some sort of photograph opportunity for its guests. This typical one at Goldrush Junction proves that the saloon girls knew how to swing. (Pat Morrison collection.)

With Frank and Jesse James behind bars—at least for a few minutes—guests could relax at the show in the Lady Gay Saloon. The marshal also served as the main performer, aided by the attractive Goldrush showgirls. (Pat Morrison collection.)

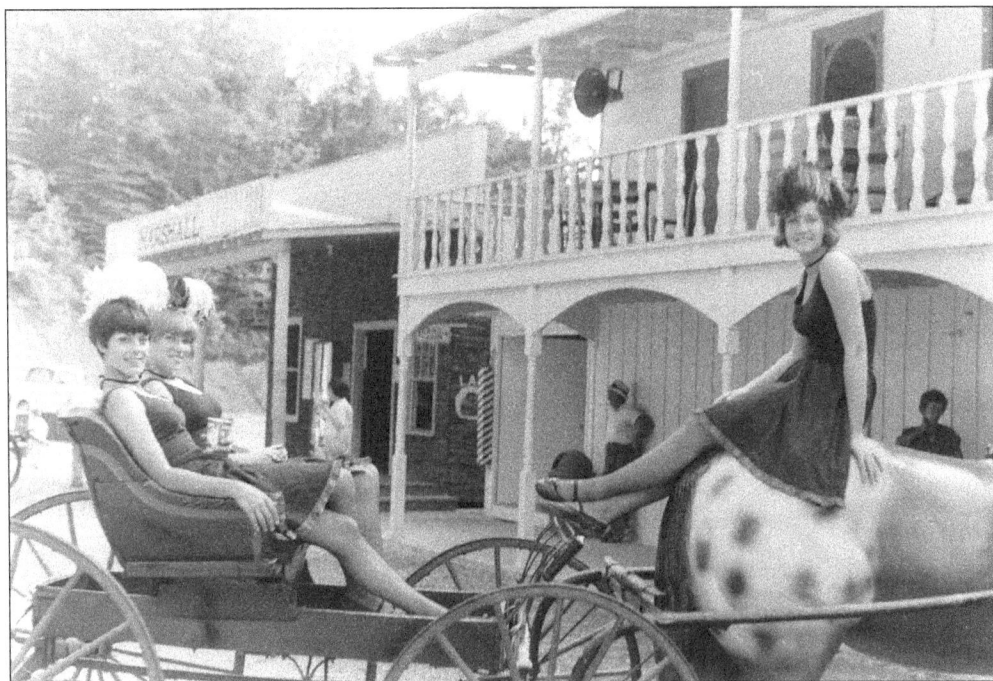

The saloon girls look happy to have their necks out of those nooses, as they take a few moments to relax before their next high-kicking performance. The horse statue partially seen here was also a part of the outlaws' comedy act, as they would break out of jail and try to make their getaway on the stationary stallion, much to kids' amusement. (Pat Morrison collection.)

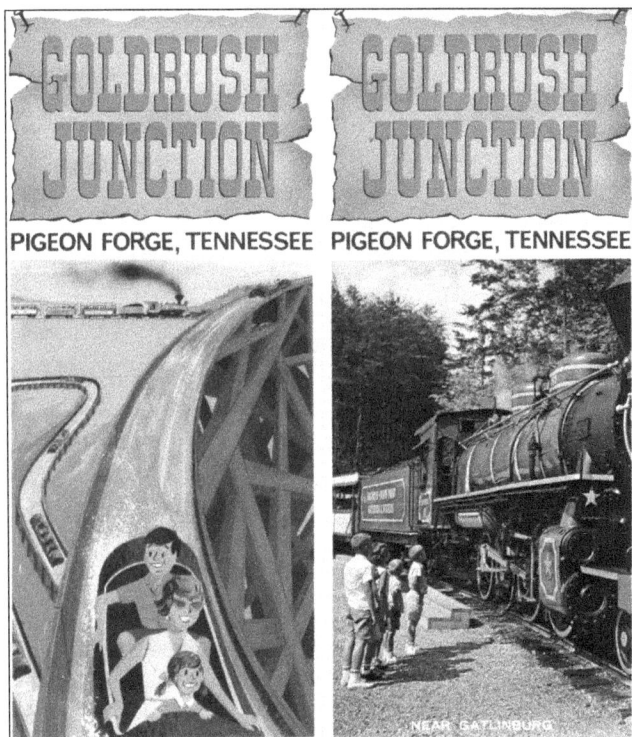

When Goldrush Junction acquired half of the log flume ride from the 1964–1965 New York World's Fair, it was really something to promote, as few people outside of that venue had ever seen one. (Tim Hollis collection.)

This aerial view shows the proximity of the new flume ride to the Goldrush Junction buildings, and some of the modifications that were taking place. Notice that the Lady Gay Saloon was now the Iron Mountain Tavern, and a few simple "umbrella rides" were beginning to cluster near the flume. (Tim Hollis collection.)

An authentic log cabin village is open to visitors who may observe craftsmen at work

The train ride back into the mountains is interrupted by an exciting attack from the renegade Harpe brothers

Chief Tassel of the Cherokee nation signs a treaty with Davy Crockett in the indian village of Choate

GOLDRUSH JUNCTION

An experience in Early American History
An attraction of The Cleveland Browns

After the death of Grover Robbins in 1970, his family sold Goldrush Junction to the Cleveland Browns football team. The park fumbled around for a few years, but the next owners would score a touchdown with it. (Tim Hollis collection.)

From the 5-mile train ride thru the Smokies, to the early American crafts, to hours of thrilling rides and the fabulous hamburgers, hot dogs and other fun-foods. Goldrush is a happy place! It's family-fun-at-its-finest . . . at Goldrush Amusement Park!

In April 1976, Goldrush Junction was purchased by Jack and Pete Herschend, the tycoons behind Silver Dollar City in Branson, Missouri. For a single season, the park operated as Goldrush Amusement Park, but most of the attractions remained the same. (Tim Hollis collection.)

# You haven't seen the Smokies till you've seen the new Silver Dollar City.

We've got a brand new ride — the Flooded Mine — with a surprise around every bend! You travel the dark passageways in an ore barge, trying to make your escape — before the torrents of onrushing water catch up with you.

• Mountain Music • Colorful Characters • Pioneer Crafts in Action • Unique Attractions • Street Shows • Great Smoky Mountain Scenery • Steam Train Excursion

For more information write Miss Martha Lou, Silver Dollar City, Pigeon Forge, TN 37863, or call (615) 453-4616.

## SILVER DOLLAR CITY®

Near Gatlinburg at Pigeon Forge, Tennessee

This impressive advertisement from 1977 announced the official name change from Goldrush to Silver Dollar City. Tourists might have been familiar with that name from its Missouri roots, but even if they were not, the Tennessee park was perfectly capable of surviving on its own merits. (Tim Hollis collection.)

The peace and quiet of Silver Dollar City would periodically be interrupted by the feudin' Hatfield and McCoy clans, who came down out of the hills to heckle visitors and generally make trouble. (Judy Ward collection.)

Maw Hatfield (Kate Headrick) was the ringleader of her troublemaking brood. Whereas in earlier days, the marshal had to worry himself with capturing Frank and Jesse James, at Silver Dollar City, he had his hands full trying to control these comical hillbillies. (Judy Ward collection.)

The Hatfields and McCoys came in all shapes and sizes, but none of the others were as cute as Sarrie Ellen McCoy, played here by Dee Marquize. At other times, Dee served as a saloon girl and, conversely, as Carrie Nation, who would arrive to bust up the evil drinkin' joint. (Judy Ward collection.)

The opportunity to have one's photograph taken had certainly come a long way from the nooses at Goldrush Junction. At Silver Dollar City, a whole family could get into the act, complete with props and costumes. The dad looks like a late arrival looking for the Rebel Railroad—and he forgot his pants. (Judy Ward collection.)

The Flooded Mine dark ride was a highly promoted addition for Silver Dollar City's inaugural 1977 season. Guests rode in boats through comical scenes of prisoners trying to escape the rising waters. The attraction was removed in 1998, but lives on in the fond memories of many park guests and employees. Meanwhile, the original Flooded Mine ride at Silver Dollar City in Missouri continues its successful run to this day. (Judy Ward collection.)

The entrance to Silver Dollar City was in the same location, and incorporated the same props, as its predecessors. By the time of this photograph, the former Cross Ties Restaurant had been converted into an administration building. (Judy Ward collection.)

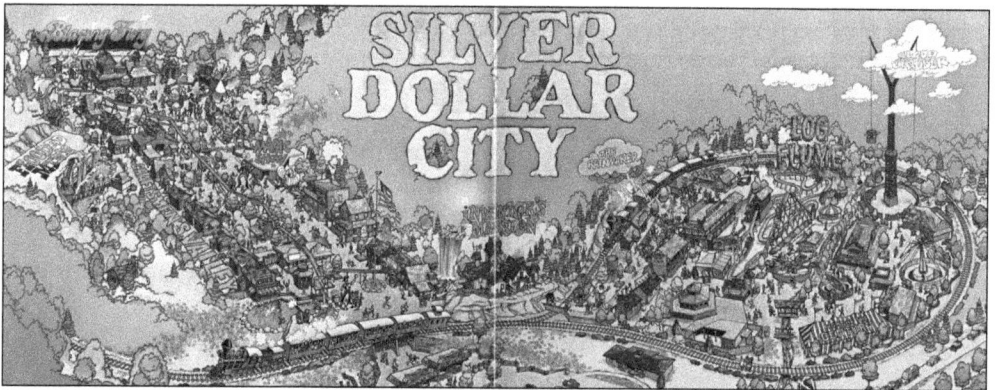

This spread shows how far the ever-expanding Silver Dollar City property had come from its beginnings. In July 1985, the Herschends made the formal announcement that Sevier County-girl-made-good Dolly Parton would become a partner in the park, and the new name would be Dollywood. The rest, to coin a cliché, is history. (Tim Hollis collection.)

68

# Four

# CELEBRITIES, REAL AND OTHERWISE

There might never have been a Dollywood if not for supermarket owner Cas Walker. He was a local celebrity in his own right for the broadcasts of his outspoken political opinions, and his television show in Knoxville was the musical debut for young Miss Parton. This example of one of Walker's grocery stores was in Dolly's hometown of Sevierville. (Mitzi Soward collection.)

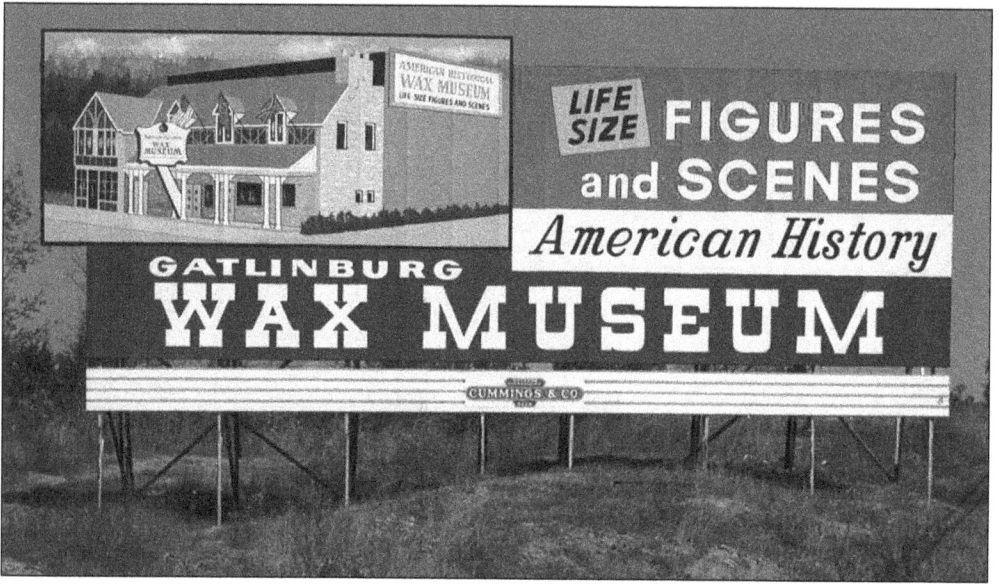

Not all of Sevier County's celebrities were as alive as Cas Walker. The American Historical Wax Museum, housed in Gatlinburg's former movie theater building, immortalized 200 years of the USA's heroes and villains. (Tim Hollis collection.)

Those who were expecting to see a Daniel Boone who looked like Fess Parker were sorely disappointed at the Gatlinburg wax museum. Boone also appears to be keeping a safe distance from that bear. (Tim Hollis collection.)

From the expressions on Mr. and Mrs. Lincoln's faces, one would never suspect that it was a comedy they were watching on the stage below, just before John Wilkes Booth gave it a big finish. (Tim Hollis collection.)

# President Jimmy Carter Is In Gatlinburg This Week!

In Life-Like Full Animation. Don't Miss This Extraordinary Display Of The 39th President Of The United States Of America, Plus Over 130 Legendary People Including: Daniel Boone, Dwight D. Eisenhower, And Elvis Presley At Gatlinburg's Wax Museum.

Open 8 A.M. To 11 P.M.

Daily

Gatlinburg's

# WAX MUSEUM

On The Parkway - Gatlinburg, Tenn.

The American Historical Wax Museum wanted to prove that it was not limited to moldy old relics of the past, so in 1978, the current occupant of the Oval Office made an animatronic appearance on the premises. (Tim Hollis collection.)

The same company that operated the American Historical Wax Museum later opened Stars Over Gatlinburg to pay tribute to the many entertainment personalities who had gained some sort of temporary or lasting fame. (Kirk Demarais collection.)

While no one could be exactly sure how true the American history figures' likenesses were to reality, this brochure makes it painfully obvious that many of the Stars Over Gatlinburg's figures bore only the slightest resemblance to their real-life counterparts. (Kirk Demarais collection.)

Although the Smoky Mountain Car Museum has been a fixture in Pigeon Forge since 1957, some of its most famous cars have now traveled to other destinations. For example, the James Bond car—yes, *the* James Bond car—along with one of Hank Williams Jr.'s vehicles, were some of the "lost attractions" once displayed therein. (Ruth Cogdill collection.)

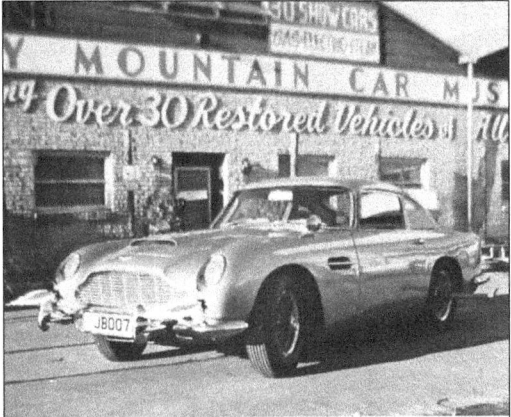

A young and debonair Jonathan Huffaker was fortunate that his grandmother worked at the Smoky Mountain Car Museum for many years. This afforded him the opportunity to pose with some really cool cars for those prom and special-occasion photographs. (Ruth Cogdill collection.)

ARCHIE CAMPBELL PRESENTS

STARS OF THE GRAND OLE OPRY

COME ANYTIME
Monday Thru Saturday
OPEN – June 14 thru Sept. 2

BIG CONTINUOUS SHOW EACH NIGHT 8:30 P.M. – 10:30 P.M.
At Craft Center, 3 Blocks from C. of C. Bldg., Hwy. 73

AUTHENTIC COUNTRY MUSIC from NASHVILLE Every Night at GATLINBURG, TENN.
LOCATED 2 BLOCKS
EAST ON HWY. 73
FROM CHAMBER OF
COMMERCE AND
LIGHT NO. 3

LIVE ACTION
Top Rate Performers
On Stage

Cast Of Stars
Appearing Nightly
At Heritage Hall

archie campbell's HEE HAW show
and GRAND OLE OPRY performers

Internationally known, Television and Recording Star, Archie Campbell presents a HEE HAW type variety show... A full evening of entertainment for the entire family... Come out tonight, or any night, except Sunday, and see a Great Show...

NOW OPEN

Showtime 8:30pm. MON. thru SAT.
SHOWING NOW THRU OCT. 30
Ramada Inn Convention Center
in Gatlinburg
Reserve seats on sale at RAMADA INN
& Many Other Locations

Although comedian Archie Campbell was not a native of Sevier County, he certainly made the region his adopted home beginning in the 1960s. In this 1968 advertisement, he was busy bringing some of his fellow *Grand Ole Opry* stars to Gatlinburg's Heritage Hall. (Tim Hollis collection.)

Ten years after his Heritage Hall shows, Campbell had moved his act to the Ramada Inn in Gatlinburg. He made it a point to appear on stage in person whenever his television schedule allowed. (Tim Hollis collection.)

By the early 1980s, Campbell had outgrown standard meeting rooms and built his own mini-theme park, Hee Haw Village, alongside US 441 in Pigeon Forge. (Tim Hollis collection.)

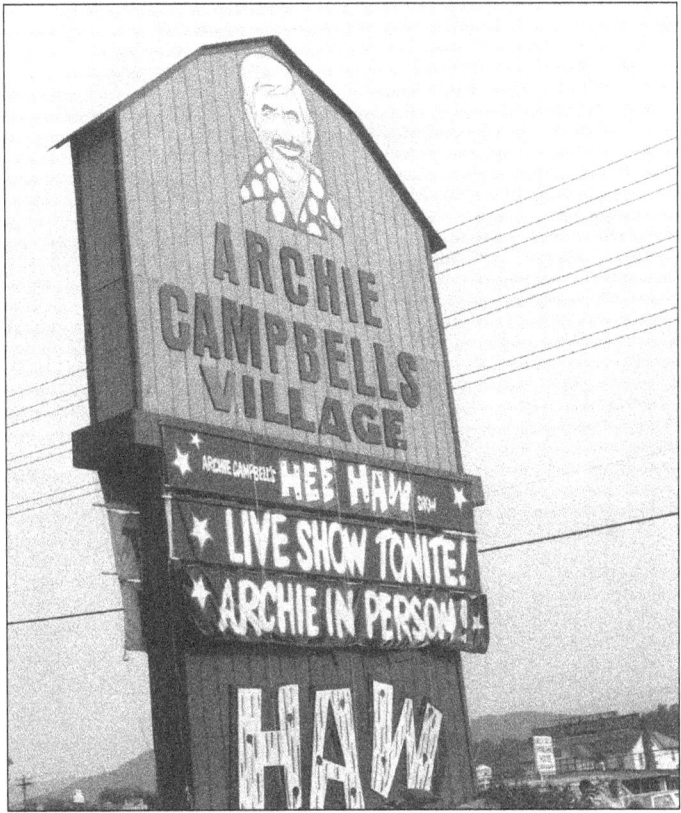

Visitors to Hee Haw Village were greeted at the entrance by this intricate statue of Archie driving the television show's trademark mule. (Tim Hollis collection.)

Archie Campbell's Hee Haw Village recreated some of the set pieces familiar from the cornpone TV show. After Campbell's death in 1987, his son Phil kept the shows going until 1994, when he sold the property. The Comedy Barn, one of Pigeon Forge's most-advertised live shows, now sits on the former site of Hee Haw Village. (Tim Hollis collection.)

Playwright Kermit Hunter was already renowned for his drama of the Cherokee Indians, *Unto These Hills*. In 1957, he produced another epic on the Tennessee side of the mountains, *Chucky Jack*, the story of John Sevier, the first governor of the state. (Tim Hollis collection.)

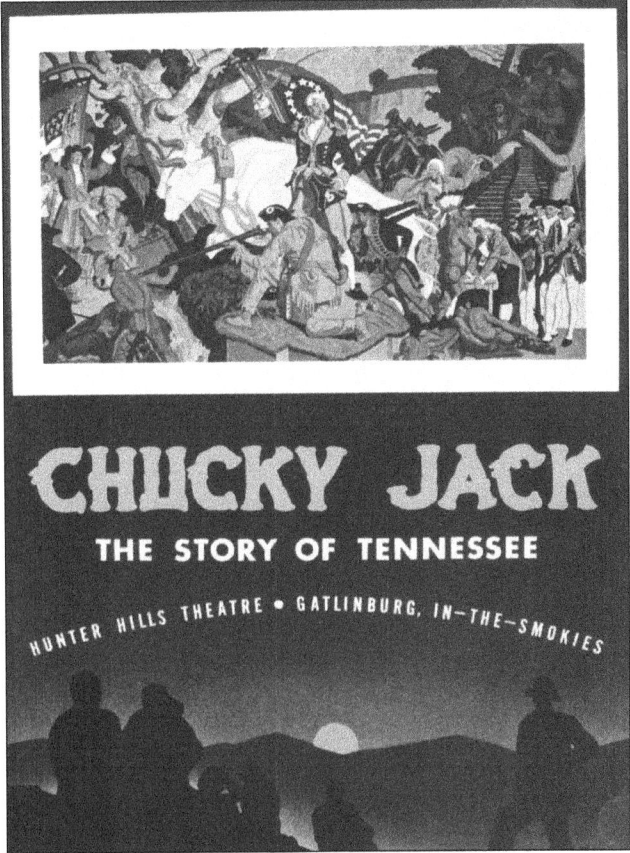

The producers of *Chucky Jack* had the unusual promotional scheme of running a miniature train through the streets of Gatlinburg, picking up tourists, and shuttling them to the outdoor amphitheater where the play was performed. (Tim Hollis collection.)

After it was curtains for *Chucky Jack*, the amphitheater was donated to the University of Tennessee, which continued to call it the Hunter Hills Theater (for Kermit Hunter, of course). Many more plays would be performed there over the following years. (Jerry Loveday collection.)

In Gatlinburg . . .  . . . Under The Stars
THE UNIVERSITY OF TENNESSEE
PRESENTS THREE SPECTACULAR STAGE PRODUCTIONS
CAMELOT • DARK OF THE MOON • EVERYMAN
HUNTER HILLS THEATRE
TENNESSEE'S LARGEST and MOST UNIQUE OUTDOOR AMPHITHEATRE
CHILDREN UNDER 6 FREE
ADULTS — $2.00
STUDENTS (Through College) — $1.00
COLORFUL COSTUMED
40 MEMBER CAST
CURTAIN TIME 8:30 P M
ON HIGHWAY 73 LESS THAN 5 MILES
FROM DOWNTOWN GATLINBURG

Beginning in the mid-1990s, there was a brief craze for big-name celebrity theaters in Pigeon Forge. It began with Dolly Parton's Music Mansion in 1994. Even though the building has now been converted into the Wonderworks museum, this sign remains on the back wall, probably forgotten even by the property's owners. (Tim Hollis collection.)

# THE SMOKIES' BEST
# RESTAURANT

A TRIBUTE TO COUNTRY MUSIC

## ALABAMA GRILL

This is ALABAMA's tribute to all the great Country Music Stars & Legends. We house the World's Largest collection of priceless memorabilia & personal artifacts honoring Country Music Stars from the Past & Present.

A TRIBUTE TO COUNTRY MUSIC

Their home was in Alabama, but the eponymous country music group made a second home for themselves in Pigeon Forge's growing celebrity neighborhood. Obviously there was some hope that Pigeon Forge could develop into another Branson, Missouri, but that was not to be. There were just too many other activities, not to mention breathtaking scenery, to divert tourists' attention from lavish stage productions. The Alabama Grill is now home to Tony Roma's Pizza. (Tim Hollis collection.)

Lee Greenwood was proud to be an American, and everyone hoped the red, white, and blue could keep his namesake theater in the black. However, today the impressive hilltop edifice serves as the New Hope Church. (Tim Hollis collection.)

The final survivor of the celebrity shows was Louise Mandrell's, which hung in there until December 31, 2005. Now known as the Miracle Theater, it still hosts a stage production, but without requiring Nashville or Hollywood star power. (Tim Hollis collection.)

Husband-and-wife team Bonnie Lou and Buster were fixtures of Knoxville television, but during the peak of the summer tourist season they would bring their "Smoky Mountain Hayride" show to theaters in Sevier County. (Mitzi Soward collection.)

Homer Harris was a renowned radio and country music star, and even appeared in Hollywood movies. He was known as the "seven-foot singing cowboy," even though he was only six-foot-five (he explained that his boots and hat brought him to the seven-foot mark). By the time of this 1970s photograph, his fame had faded, and he was playing his guitar and posing for photographs in front of an unidentified Pigeon Forge pancake house. (Tim Johnson collection.)

# Five

# PRE-HYSTERICAL FUN

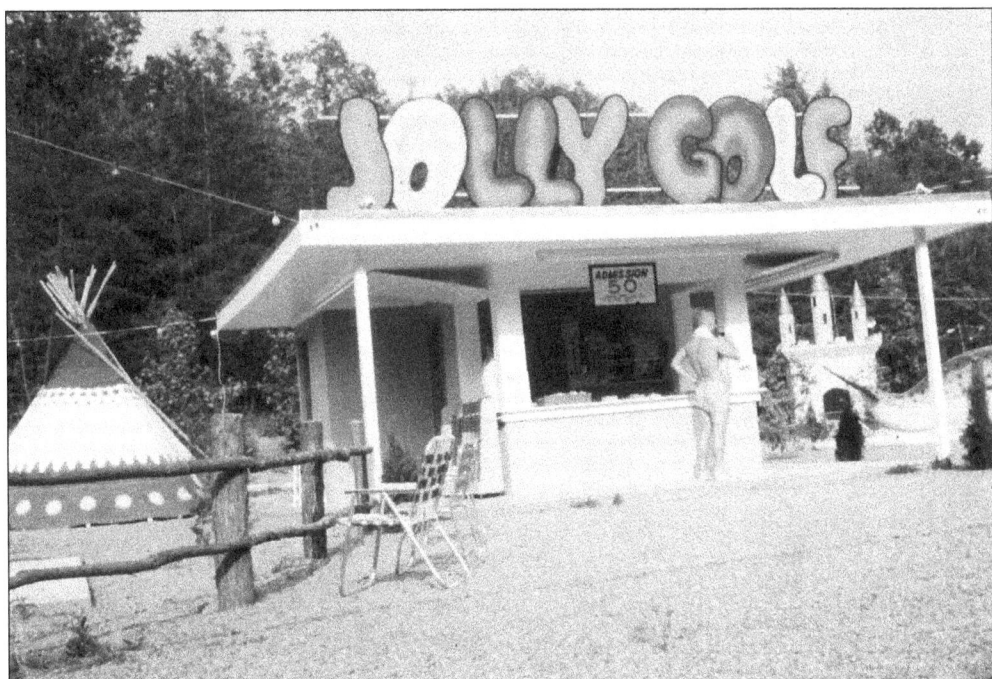

In 1961, Murfreesboro businessmen Richard Craddock and Jim Sidwell teamed up to build Jolly Golf in Gatlinburg. It was the first in a long line of Smokies attractions with giant statues of prehistoric creatures and other colorful varmints. (Becky Craddock collection.)

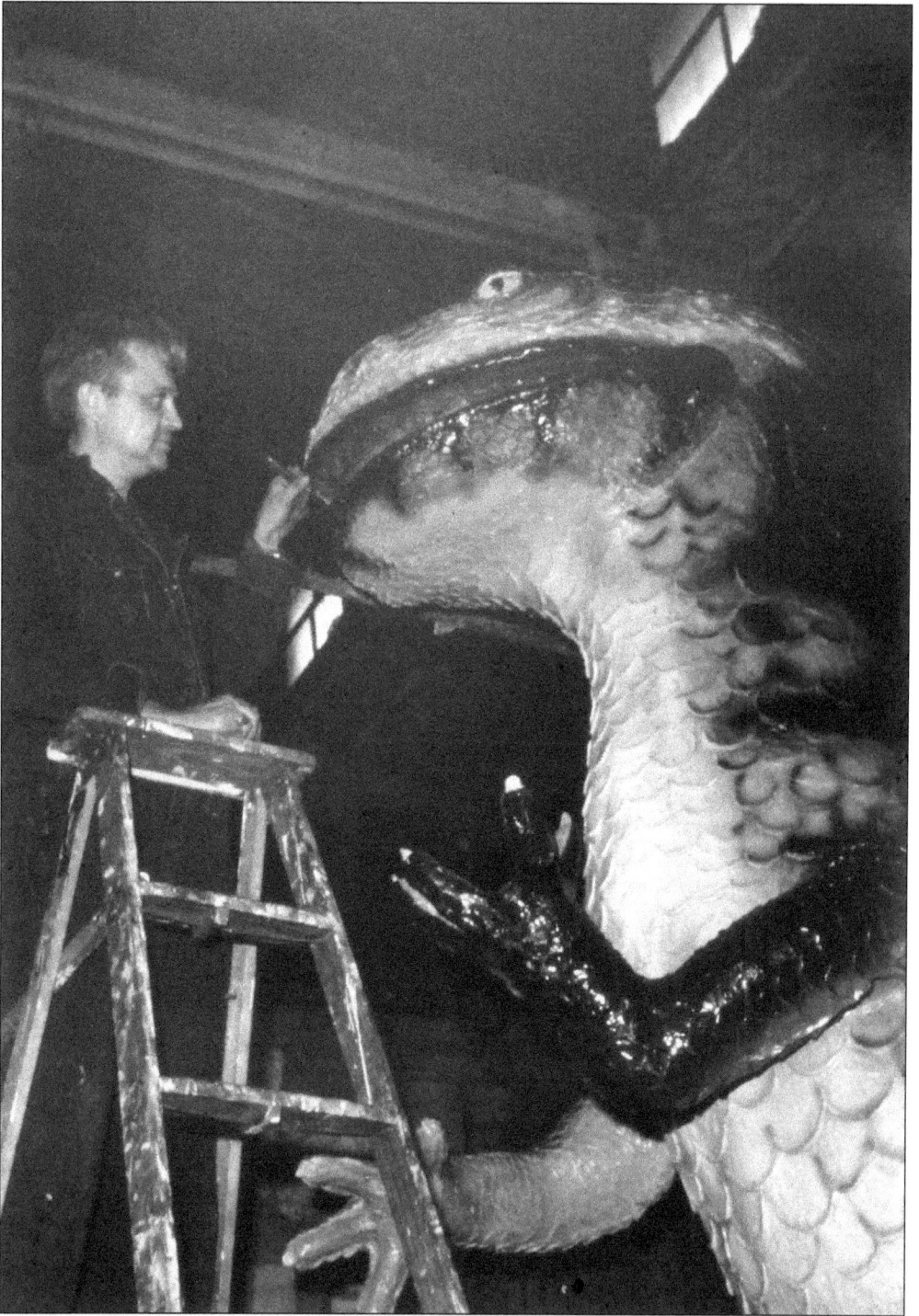

This is one of the only known photographs of Jim Sidwell working on one of the future Jolly Golf obstacles. The figures were crafted in Sidwell and Craddock's warehouse in Murfreesboro and then transported by flatbed truck over to Gatlinburg—eliciting some funny looks from other highway travelers along the way. (Becky Craddock collection.)

Once in place, Sidwell's tyrannosaurus looked a bit potbellied, as if he might have just finished a meal of a brontosaurus or two. (Becky Craddock collection.)

Jolly Golf was admittedly inspired by the look of the dinosaur-and-windmill style of miniature golf courses that had recently sprung up along Florida's Miracle Strip, particularly Goofy Golf and Zoo-Land Golf in Panama City Beach. (Becky Craddock collection.)

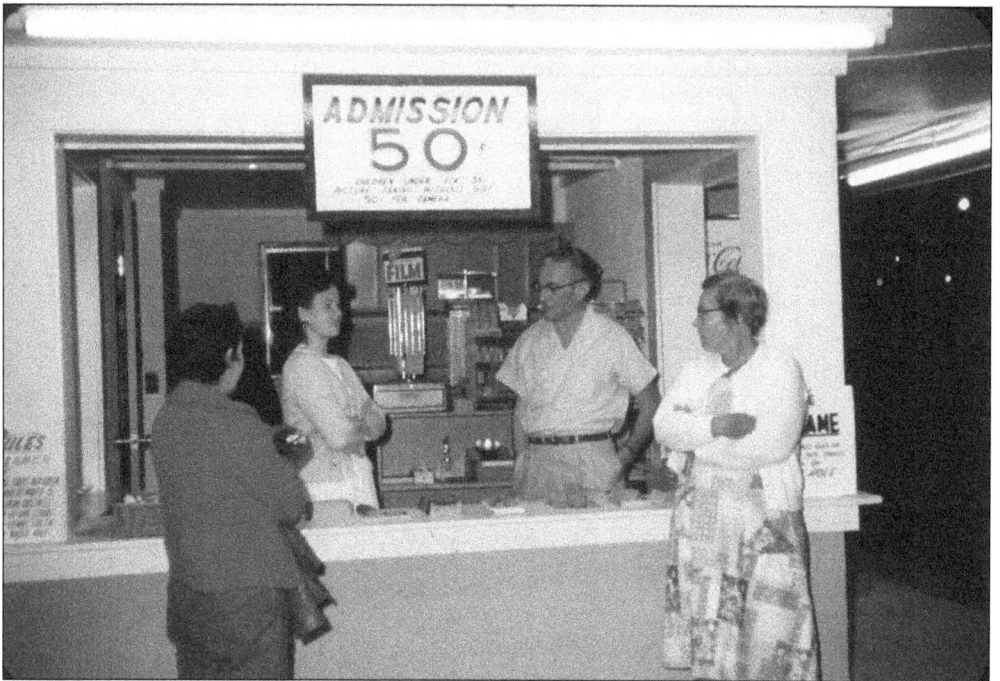

In 1961, it would set visitors back half a buck to play 18 holes of Jolly Golf. In the fine print, notice that the same rate applied for people who wanted to take photographs without engaging in the game. (Becky Craddock collection.)

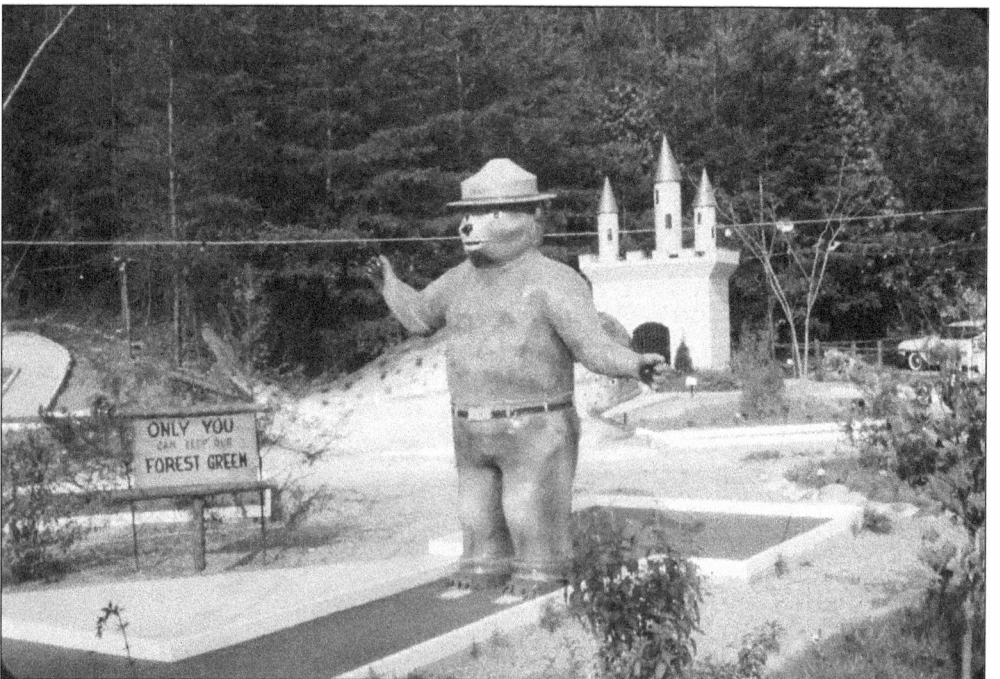

Jolly Golf originally featured this Smokey Bear replica that waved its right arm up and down. As with the case of the Smoky Cub Motel we saw earlier, the US Forest Service eventually curtailed such unauthorized use of their valuable trademark. (Becky Craddock collection.)

Richard Craddock sold out his interest in Jolly Golf in the mid-1960s, but Jim Sidwell kept enlarging the course over the next decade. He eventually maintained an entire "dinosaur factory" in Murfreesboro just to turn out figures for miniature golf courses and other roadside attractions. (Tim Hollis collection.)

Originally, Jolly Golf had only 18 holes, but after Sidwell became sole owner, it expanded up the hill behind the original layout and added a second 18-hole collection of figures. (Rod Bennett collection.)

The Wise Old Owl was one of the original 1961 characters at Jolly Golf, but the giant behemoth known as Big Bronto, seen in the background, was one of the later immigrants. (Tim Hollis collection.)

Not everything at Jolly Golf dealt with prehistoric life. This giant fairy-tale shoe was one of the obstacles that showed Sidwell's more whimsical side. (Tim Hollis collection.)

Perhaps Linus's annual search for the Great Pumpkin would have come to a happier ending if he had encountered this giant specimen at Jolly Golf. (Tim Hollis collection.)

This overview of Jolly Golf was taken in 1985. Notice that the former Smokey Bear had received a new coat of shaggy black fur and a hillbilly hat, and was known as Ol' Pokey Bear. An original 1961 whale and tepee were sharing space with later arrivals Big Bronto and the Biggest Nut in Tennessee. (Tim Hollis collection.)

In the late 1990s, the Sidwell family revamped Jolly Golf, removing any of the figures that were not prehistoric, and renaming it Dinosaur Golf. (Notice that the 1961 tyrannosaurus had been replaced by a less well-fed version, too.) After Dinosaur Golf became extinct in 2004, the property sat empty for a while before being developed into today's Davy Crockett Mini-Golf, a project of the vast Ripley organization. (Tim Hollis collection.)

Miniature golf really took hold along the main drag in Pigeon Forge, where more property was available than in congested Gatlinburg. Safari Golf was an example of the typical 1980s approach, which used prefabricated fiberglass figures instead of handcrafted obstacles. (Tim Hollis collection.)

There is still a course known as Fantasy Golf in Pigeon Forge, but the simple figures in this 1985 photograph have been replaced by gigantic dragons, mermaids, and other oversized mythological fauna. (Tim Hollis collection.)

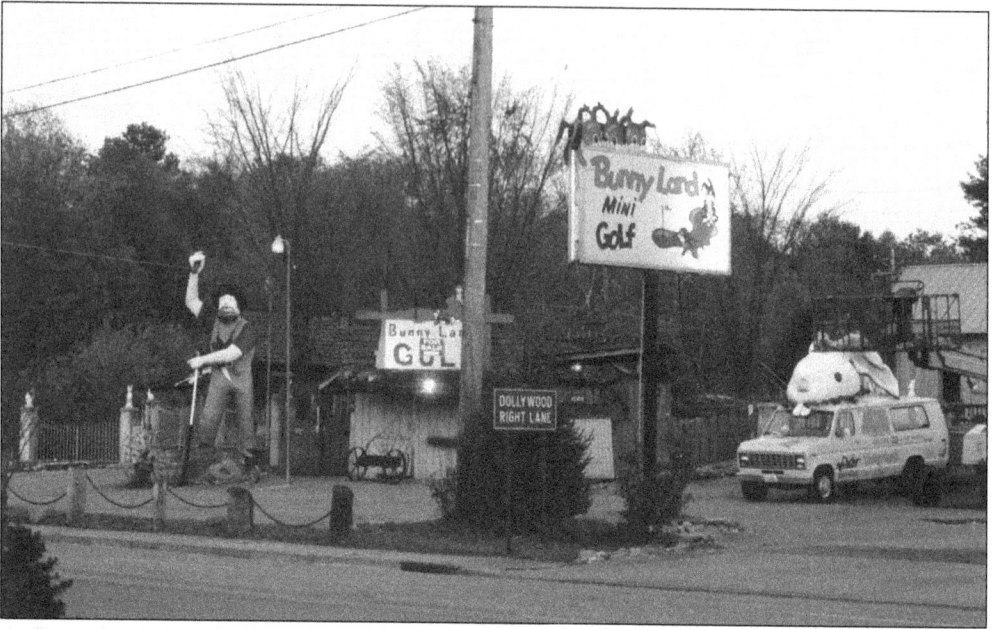

At Bunnyland Mini-Golf, on the road leading to the entrance to Dollywood, players putted their way around a herd of live rabbits. The property became infamous for the not-so-happy fate of its long-eared residents, as detailed in the lurid documentary film, titled simply *Bunnyland*. (Tim Hollis collection.)

After the bunnies bit the dust—literally—the course took on the perhaps more appropriate name Nightmare Mini-Golf. The remnants of this enterprise now sit overgrown with weeds and foliage, awaiting the next chapter in its strange story. (Tim Hollis collection.)

The one constant through the ill-fated Bunnyland/Nightmare Mini-Golf saga has been this giant figure at the entrance. These oversized pioneers can be found in many different locations along the American roadside, but a sitting version was originally the emblem of a forgotten chain of 1960s drive-in hamburger joints known as Wagon Ho. Their buildings were made to resemble giant Conestoga wagons, and these Gabby Hayes look-alikes were mounted on the buckboard as if driving an invisible team of horses. (Tim Hollis collection.)

Enjoy **SIGHTSEEING** the

# MAGIC WORLD

**THE MOST UNUSUAL TOUR OF A LIFETIME**

Ride the **BASHMOBILES**

Play **MAGIC CARPET GOLF**

Gifts from the **THIEVES MARKET**

**BEHIND THE VOLCANO AT NORTH END OF PIGEON FORGE NEXT TO CAR MUSEUM**

**DAY & NIGHT SPECTACULAR**

Meanwhile, Jim Sidwell was expanding his dinosaur-based empire far beyond Jolly Golf. In 1972, he opened his own theme park, Magic World, in Pigeon Forge. (Jim Sidwell Jr. collection.)

Magic World contained not only one of Sidwell's trademark miniature golf courses, but a range of other activities including a walk through the dark tunnels of a concrete volcano and a train ride back through time. (Jim Sidwell Jr. collection.)

**THE WORLD AND ITS OTHER LIFE !**

THE WORLD UNDER WATER !

MAGIC WORLD on U.S. 441
at Pigeon Forge, Tennessee
You've got to See It to Believe It !
Bring Your Camera
For a Thrill to Remember !

THE WORLD OF THE CAVEMEN !

"Ride the DRAGON TRAIN through DINOSAUR CANYON back to the Beginning of Time"

# UNBELIEVABLE
## the Magnificent Journey thru
### *Magic World*

- CAVEMAN CITY -
- GHOST GROTTO -
- DRAGON TRAIN RIDE -
- DINOSAUR CANYON -
- INVISIBLE PEOPLE -
- UNDERWATER WORLD AQUARIUM -
- ABOMINABLE SNOWMAN -

**AND MUCH, MUCH MORE!**

This 1974 brochure gives some rare views of Magic World's earliest attractions, including the miniature golf course (center). Although it was similar to some tourist sites in Florida, nothing like Magic World had ever been seen in the Smokies. (Tim Hollis collection.)

Magic World Map — The Magnificent Journey

This handy map shows the layout of the original Magic World property. After entering through the pirate ship, visitors tramped through the volcano's musty corridors, where a series of tableaux could be viewed through windows. The Abominable Snowman hung out in one grotto, while another contained the Invisible Man (only his glowing, fluorescent hat and gloves indicated his presence). In another scene, the ghost of a prospector—or maybe a pros-*specter*—chipped away at a stone wall, while his decomposing skeleton lay on the ground. (Tim Hollis collection.)

No self-respecting theme park would be without its own costumed character, so Magic World had Dizzy Dinosaur stationed near the entrance to make kids' heads swim. (Tim Hollis collection.)

Magic World's Dragon Train promoted its experience as "an educational museum of prehistoric life." It could just as well have been called "Jim Sidwell's catalog brought to life," as it featured examples of most of the different figures he was producing in his Murfreesboro factory. (Tim Hollis collection.)

A trip through the Magic World volcano was climaxed by a ride aboard the Earth Auger, a compartment inside a rotating drum that gave the sensation of burrowing deep into the earth's core. Upon alighting, visitors were confronted by this Satanic inhabitant, with a continuous recorded spiel welcoming them to his home and suggesting that they might want to stay forever. (Cliff Holman collection.)

In the mid-1970s, Magic World began getting away from its prehistoric theme. On the hill in the background, notice the park's new Flying Saucer attraction, a 360-degree theater that simulated flying over the Smokies' autumn splendor. (Cliff Holman collection.)

While Gatlinburg would soon be cloning Disney's Country Bear Jamboree at two different attractions, in 1978, Magic World got into the act first with its animatronic Confederate Critters show, starring Gen. Cornelius Bearpatch, Col. Mosby Greyhound III, and Maj. Stonewall J. Fox. (Rod Bennett collection.)

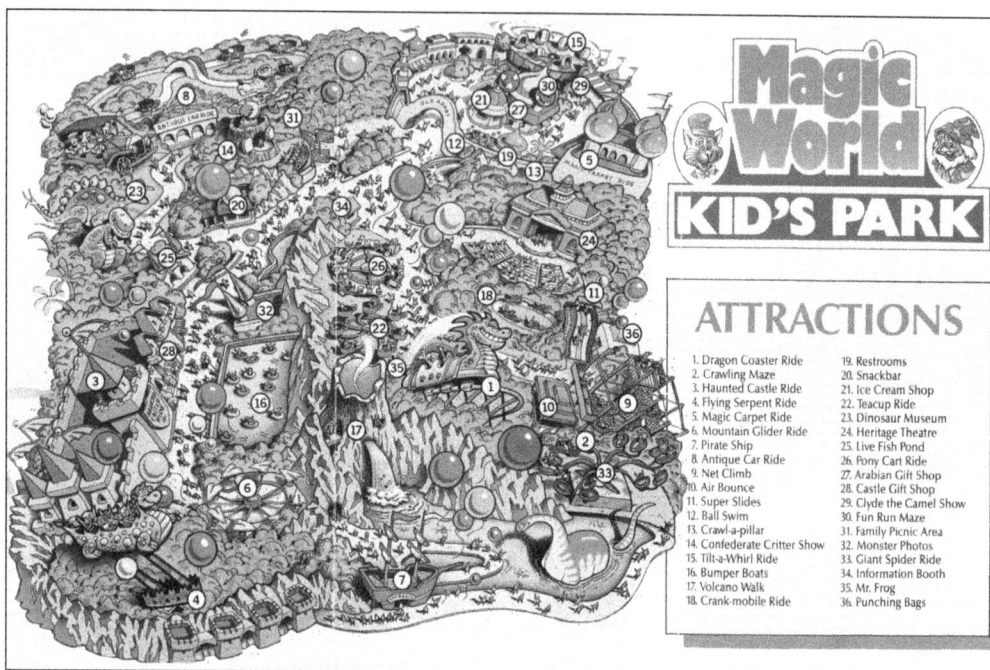

Magic World KID'S PARK

## ATTRACTIONS

| | |
|---|---|
| 1. Dragon Coaster Ride | 19. Restrooms |
| 2. Crawling Maze | 20. Snackbar |
| 3. Haunted Castle Ride | 21. Ice Cream Shop |
| 4. Flying Serpent Ride | 22. Teacup Ride |
| 5. Magic Carpet Ride | 23. Dinosaur Museum |
| 6. Mountain Glider Ride | 24. Heritage Theatre |
| 7. Pirate Ship | 25. Live Fish Pond |
| 8. Antique Car Ride | 26. Pony Cart Ride |
| 9. Net Climb | 27. Arabian Gift Shop |
| 10. Air Bounce | 28. Castle Gift Shop |
| 11. Super Slides | 29. Clyde the Camel Show |
| 12. Ball Swim | 30. Fun Run Maze |
| 13. Crawl-a-pillar | 31. Family Picnic Area |
| 14. Confederate Critter Show | 32. Monster Photos |
| 15. Tilt-a-Whirl Ride | 33. Giant Spider Ride |
| 16. Bumper Boats | 34. Information Booth |
| 17. Volcano Walk | 35. Mr. Frog |
| 18. Crank-mobile Ride | 36. Punching Bags |

Compare this 1985 map with the one back on page 96 to see just how much Magic World had expanded and changed its theme by that time. The original Volcano Walk and dinosaurs were almost lost among all the new activities. (Tim Hollis collection.)

While it had always been aimed at children, the new theme at Magic World placed it more squarely in the kids' playground realm. It is hard to criticize that, though, when the kids are as cute as these. (Tim Hollis collection.)

The "new, improved" Magic World featured regularly scheduled magic shows by Merlin Rainbow, who must have found his art more difficult than most magicians due to being encumbered by a big cartoon head. (Tim Hollis collection.)

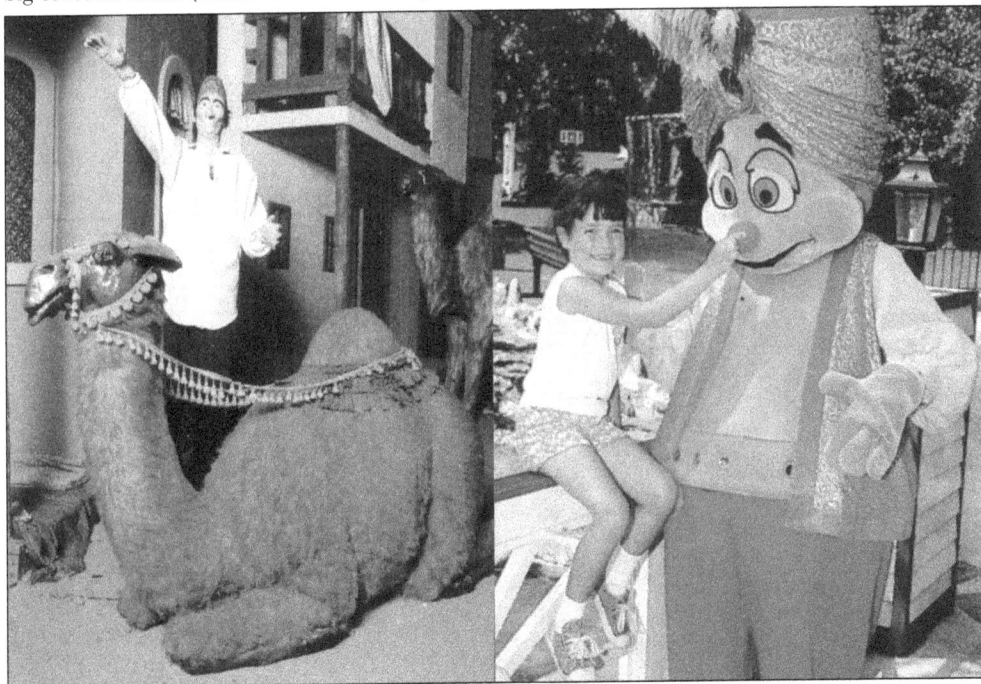

A huge new area at the back of the property was themed to an "Old Araby" motif, with appropriate costumed characters and a dark ride that sent visitors back to the days of Ali Baba aboard flying carpets suspended from an overhead rail. (Tim Hollis collection.)

After the 1995 season, Magic World took a bow and disappeared. By the time of this April 1998 photograph, the property had been mostly cleared. This remaining strange shape was formerly the exit from the Volcano Walk. (Tim Hollis collection.)

In 1999, the Sidwell family opened a new miniature golf course, Professor Hacker's Lost Treasure Golf, on the former Magic World property. Its ship and volcano are not the same ones that graced the entrance to Magic World, but serve to remind everyone of what used to be on the site. (Tim Hollis collection.)

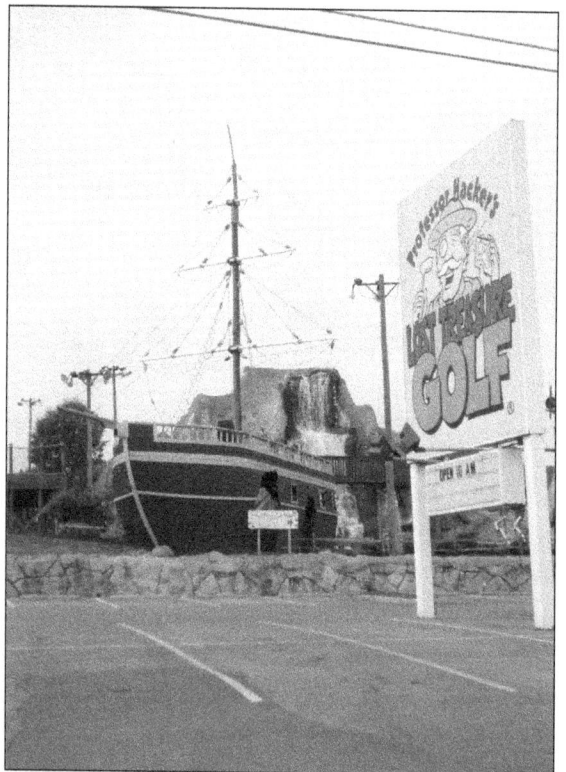

## Six

# BELIEVE IT OR DON'T

There has been a Ripley's *Believe It or Not!* Museum in Gatlinburg since 1968. However, visitors can no longer visit the building seen here because it burned in the same 1992 fire that turned the Rebel Corner souvenir store into a lost cause. This chapter features a number of other attractions that somehow just did not seem to fit their Smokies locale. (Tim Hollis collection.)

# Don't Miss
# Fort Weare Game Park

*Animal Wonderland Of*

*The Great Smokies*

PIGEON FORGE, TENN.

On U. S. 441 — Six Miles North of Gatlinburg

One of Pigeon Forge's earliest attractions was the Fort Weare Game Park, a roadside zoo established in the 1950s. Many years later, the site traded its live animals for the artificial variety when Magic World was built on the same property. (Tim Hollis collection.)

Long after Fort Weare, another petting zoo came to Pigeon Forge with the straightforward name Baby Animal Kingdom. The baby animals could no doubt out-cute any of the baby humans that came to see them. (Tim Hollis collection.)

BABY ANIMAL KINGDOM

A Thrill For The Young & Old

A Must For Children!

See Our Kingdom Of Baby Animals And Farm Yard Petting Area.
Open Thru Oct. 23   9:30 a.m. - 9:30 p.m.
Pigeon Forge, Tenn (Hwy. 441 - Parkway)
Located Across From Mountain Ocean

SWIM IN REAL OCEAN WAVES!

Mountain Ocean
WAVE POOL

PIGEON FORGE, TN.

Mountain Ocean
THE MOST EXCITING NEW RECREATION FACILITY IN THE SMOKIES. IT'S THE FUN PLACE FOR KIDS OF ALL AGES
See It All
WAVE POOL • ARCADE • GIFT SHOP • ICE CREAM PARLOR • FAST FOODS • INDIAN JEWEL-RY • PHOTOGRAPHY • CANDY KITCHEN • FREE PARKING.

P. O. BOX 1109
PIGEON FORGE, TN. 37863
(615) 453-9283

Just the name "Mountain Ocean" would have made this seem like a terrifically misplaced attraction. The idea of a wave pool in the Smoky Mountains must have seemed like a good idea for at least a few years, though. (Tim Hollis collection.)

**Fabulous Fairyland**

FOR CHILDREN

Robin Hood watches as the Cat Plays the Fiddle for
Little Miss Muffet and Little Boy Blue

Most Beautiful Show For
Children In The Mountains

ON U. S. HIGHWAY 441 IN
PIGEON FORGE, TENNESSEE
Five Miles North of Gatlinburg

The collection of animated figures known as Fairyland was a Pigeon Forge fixture beginning in the late 1950s. The scenes were similar to department store window animation, portraying scenes from famous fairy tales and nursery rhymes, with an unauthorized guest appearance by Mickey Mouse and other members of the Disney gang. (Tim Hollis collection.)

Fairyland tended to indiscriminately mix characters from various stories. In this scene, Goldilocks and the Three Bears were joined by Wee Willie Winkie, running through the town, upstairs, downstairs, in his nightgown. (Tim Hollis collection.)

In another example of character crossover, the Fairyland "goody shop" featured Mother Goose and Bobby Shaftoe serving refreshments to Little Boy Blue and Little Miss Muffet. (Tim Hollis collection.)

Boy Blue and Miss Muffet were obviously becoming a Fairyland version of a Hollywood couple; in this scene, they could be found dancing together to the music of the Cat and the Fiddle. No one could figure out why Robin Hood, on the hill above, seemed to find this so hilarious. (Tim Hollis collection.)

Of course, everyone remembers the tale in which the Three Blind Mice met Rapunzel, don't they? No? Oh well, that was Fairyland's story, and they were sticking to it. (Tim Hollis collection.)

After Fairyland closed in the mid-1970s, its collection of animated figures was dispersed among a number of Sevier County businesses and private collectors. Later, a Ponderosa Steakhouse was constructed where the Fairyland building formerly sat. (Tim Hollis collection.)

Anyone interested in buying property in Fairyland? Even the Ponderosa has been sent to the last roundup, and this is how the Fairyland site appeared in the fall of 2010. No lot alongside the Pigeon Forge strip can be expected to remain vacant for long, so something else will surely come along—attracting visitors who are totally unaware of what used to exist here. (Tim Hollis collection.)

The Space Ship was a short-lived Gatlinburg attraction that could only have existed in the days before manned space travel. Sixteen visitors at a time sat in a small theater-type building and viewed their "trip to the moon" on a screen. (Jerry Loveday collection.)

Smoky Poky

A MINIATURE COAL FIRED STEAM LOCOMOTIVE WITH TENDER & CARS ON U.S. 441, 5 MI. N. OF GATLINBURG

FUN AND EXCITEMENT FOR YOUNG AND OLD
TICKETS: CHILDREN .25—ADULTS .35

See... Arrows To Atoms
Pigeon Forge, Tenn.

These two Pigeon Forge attractions are so obscure that no information appears to have survived about them. The Smoky Poky was obviously a fairly standard amusement park ride, but it is anyone's guess as to what Arrows to Atoms was. (Tim Hollis collection.)

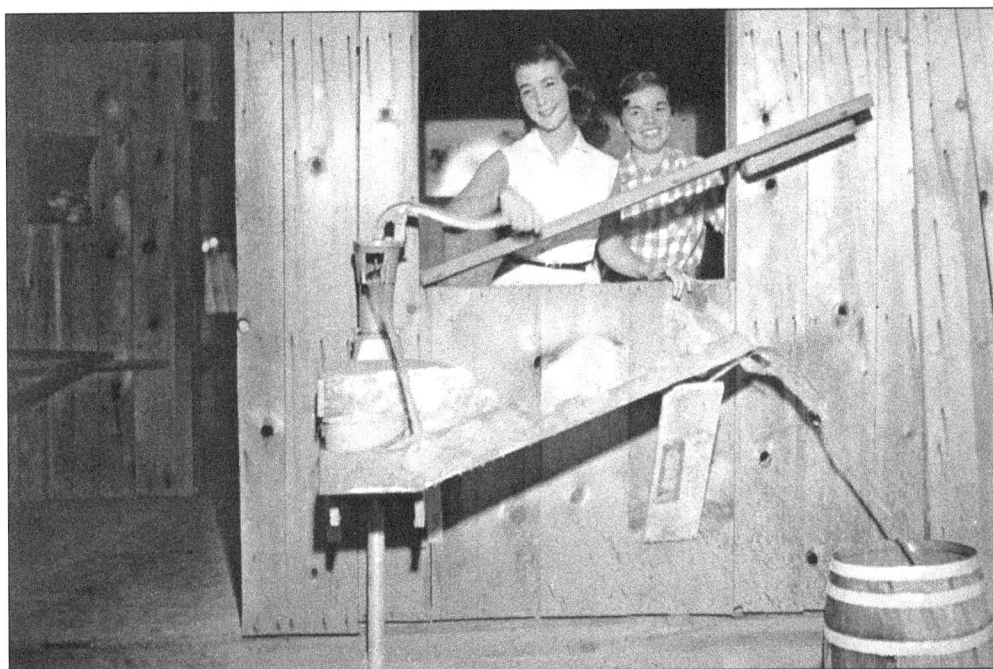

Mystery Hill was one of those traditional optical illusion houses that seemed to defy gravity. Here, two of the attractive hosts demonstrate Mystery Hill's ability to make water run uphill. (Bob Howard collection.)

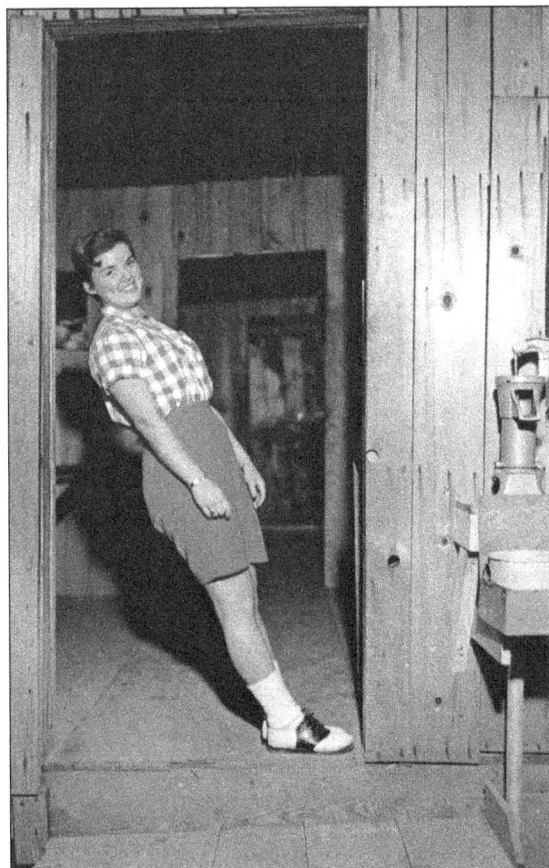

Anyone who has visited one of the scores of "mystery houses" scattered among American tourist centers has seen this routine, where a seemingly level floor makes people stand at odd angles. (Bob Howard collection.)

By the 1970s, Mystery Hill had been obliged to update its postcards with girls in more modern attire. The mysterious happenings just kept going unchanged, however, including the ability of a chair to balance on two legs against a wall. (Tim Hollis collection.)

Outside the Mystery Hill building—with only a fence separating it from Jolly Golf—these two oh-so-cool girls of the early 1970s use a pair of concrete blocks to change sizes with each other. (Tim Hollis collection.)

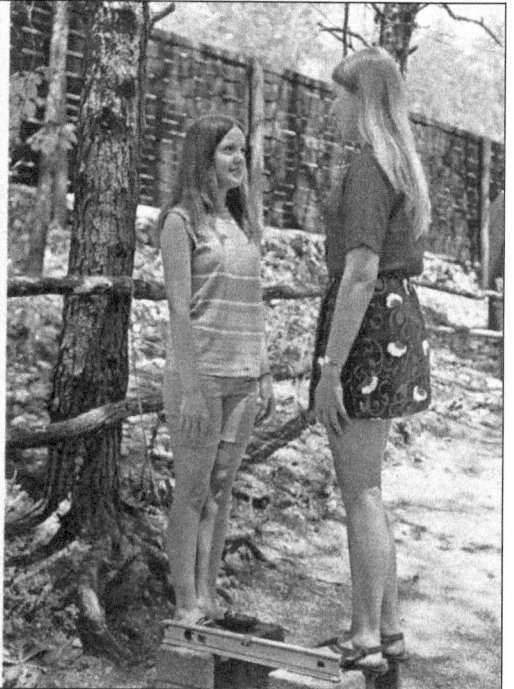

Considering that the Smokies were primarily a summer and fall tourist destination, it was surprising that Christmas became such a prevalent theme in the area. Santa's Cottage in Gatlinburg was a tiny shop, but drew attention with its sleigh and reindeer on the roof 365 days of the year. (Tim Hollis collection.)

The Christmas Tree Inc. in Gatlinburg was another of the small year-round Yuletide shops that served as forerunners to today's enormous Christmas Place store in Pigeon Forge and the Country Christmas complex in Kodak. (Tim Hollis collection.)

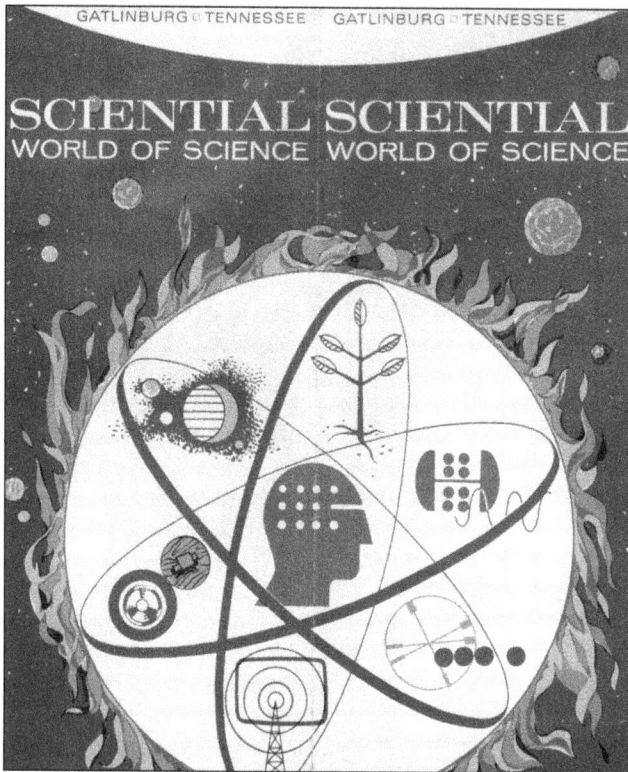

SCIENTIAL SCIENTIAL
WORLD OF SCIENCE WORLD OF SCIENCE

"Say, kids, as long as we're on vacation here in Gatlinburg, what could be more fun than visiting a science museum with a name no one can pronounce? Come on, I promise it'll be fun!" (Tim Hollis collection.)

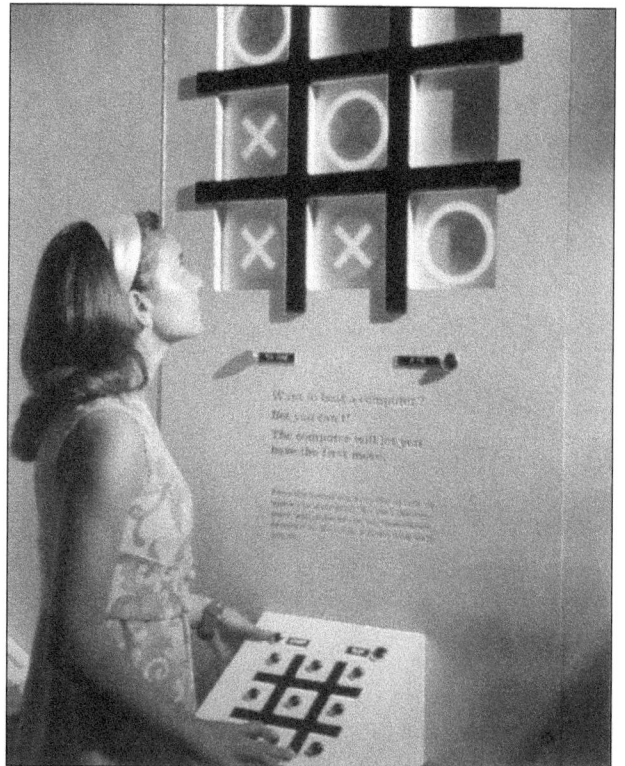

How can playing miniature golf among colorful dinosaurs, or shopping for souvenirs at Hill-Billy Village, compare to the ecstasy of playing electronic tic-tac-toe? In case the reader hasn't figured it out yet, the Sciential museum soon found that tourists were not particularly interested in its "edu-tainment" agenda. (Tim Hollis collection.)

One of Pigeon Forge's most misplaced-looking attractions came about in 1978, when Wisconsin Dells impresario Tommy Bartlett decided the Smokies resort would be a good location for a branch of his famed water-ski show. (Tim Hollis collection.)

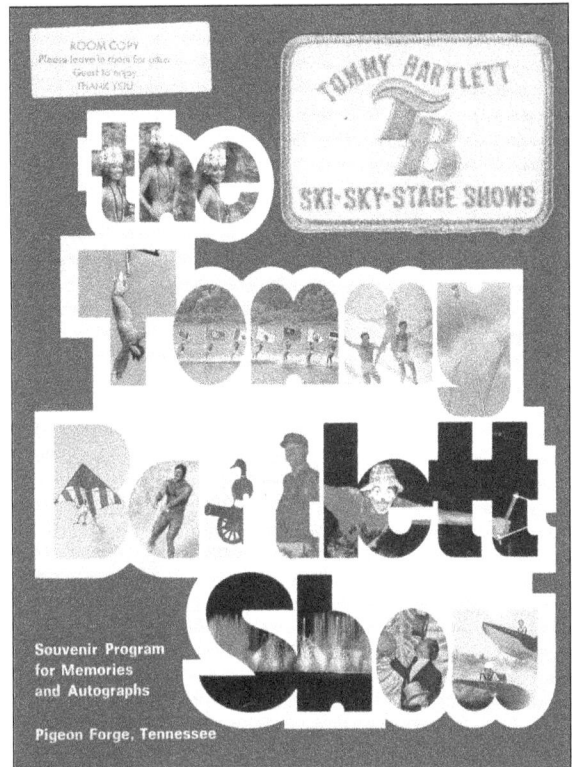

the Tommy Bartlett Show

Souvenir Program
for Memories
and Autographs

Pigeon Forge, Tennessee

TOMMY BARTLETT
TB
SKI·SKY·STAGE SHOWS

Thank you for visiting
The Tommy Bartlett Show
and come back real soon!

The fact that Pigeon Forge contained no lake large enough for water-skiing stunts was no deterrent to Tommy Bartlett. He simply dug his own lake and filled it with water and performers, with a grandstand to hold all the spectators expected to watch. (Tim Hollis collection.)

Although the Bartlett ski show operated in a truly impressive complex, it lasted only a few years. Today, the slowly rusting grandstand and seats can still be seen on a hillside just off the main Pigeon Forge strip. The former giant pool where the water-skiers performed their stunts is now a verdant patch of grass. (Tim Hollis collection.)

If anything could have looked more misplaced in the Smokies than Bartlett's water-skiers, it might have been the trained porpoise shows. The Tennessee Porpoise Circus was one of the first of these. (Tim Hollis collection.)

# Tennessee Porpoise Circus
## PIGEON FORGE, TENN.

– CHICO –

– SMOKY –

– L B J –
(Lady Bird Jumper)

First Show 9 A. M.
On The Hour Thru 5 P. M.

NIGHT SPECTACULAR
At 8:30 P. M.

—FEATURING—

THE ASTRONUT'S

COMEDY DIVING TEAM
An Exciting Underwater Show

Special
Admission Price

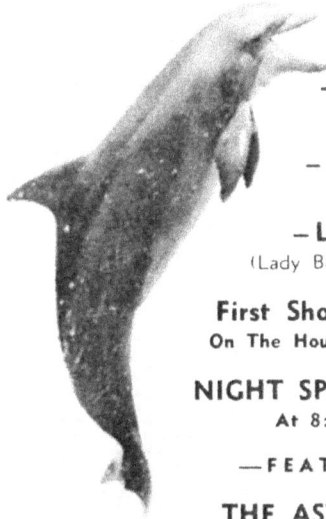

ONE ADULT FREE
WITH TWO PAYING GUESTS
TENNESSEE PORPOISE CIRCUS

FLIPPER'S
"KISSING COUSINS"
performing on the hour
9 A.M. thru 5 P.M.—Night Show 8 P.M.

Pigeon Forge, Tennessee
Highway 441
7 miles from Gatlinburg

SHOWS RAIN OR SHINE UNDER COVERED BLEACHERS

Coauthor Mitzi Soward remembers being offered the opportunity to make a guest appearance swimming with the porpoises at the Tennessee Porpoise Circus, but she decided she would rather do her swimming elsewhere. (Tim Hollis collection.)

What is this—Florida? No, it is Pigeon Forge's most fish-out-of-water attraction of all time, Porpoise Island. Despite the fact that it fit the mountain country about as well as a hillbilly band playing in Times Square, Porpoise Island is remembered fondly by the employees who worked there during its brief tenure. (Tim Hollis collection.)

Porpoise Island was an exotic oasis of Hawaiian culture in Sevier County. With its cast of entertainers, many from the islands of the Pacific, Porpoise Island was a welcome addition to the myriad of mini-golf courses and other attractions lining the highway to the Smokies. (Tim Hollis collection.)

It cannot be denied that Porpoise Island was a great benefactor for the local economy. Probably at no other time in history could so many performers of Polynesian descent have found such opportunities for gainful employment in the Smokies. (Tim Hollis collection.)

Like the Tommy Bartlett Show, Porpoise Island employed lithe young girls in itsy-bitsy bikinis to put the namesake performers through their paces. (Shelia Atchley collection.)

Besides trained porpoise shows, another attraction that tried to branch out from Florida into the Smokies was Xanadu. One of these "houses of the future" was built in Kissimmee and another in Gatlinburg. It might have been more successful than, say, the Sciential museum, but that was not saying much. The house of the future was a memory of the past by the mid-1980s. (Kirk Demarais collection.)

## VISIT GATLINBURG'S TOUR THRU HELL . . .

- See the Lake of Fire.
- See a replica of the Coin Judas received for betraying Christ.
- Walk on the Burning Brimstone.
- See the Invisible Hand with the drop of water floating thru the air.
- See Pontius Pilate's hands turn to blood before your very eyes.
- See the Wicked Jezebel and many other attractions.

And now, we arrive at the attraction that was apparently conceived as the "flip side" of Christus Gardens: the Tour Through Hell. This attraction also had the unique distinction of being the landmark to which locals referred when giving directions to the ski resort. During the short time it occupied its spot at the foot of Ski Mountain, locals often told people searching for the ski resort to "go to hell and turn right" (or left, depending on the approach). (Tim Hollis collection.)

The Tour Through Hell's founder, minister Bud Spriggs, remains as shadowy a figure as his short-lived tourist attraction. Other than his two underworld excursions in Gatlinburg and Hell, Michigan (where else?), his only other notable endeavor seems to have been a 1960s record album in which he explained that UFOs were related to the Book of Revelation. (Tim Hollis collection.)

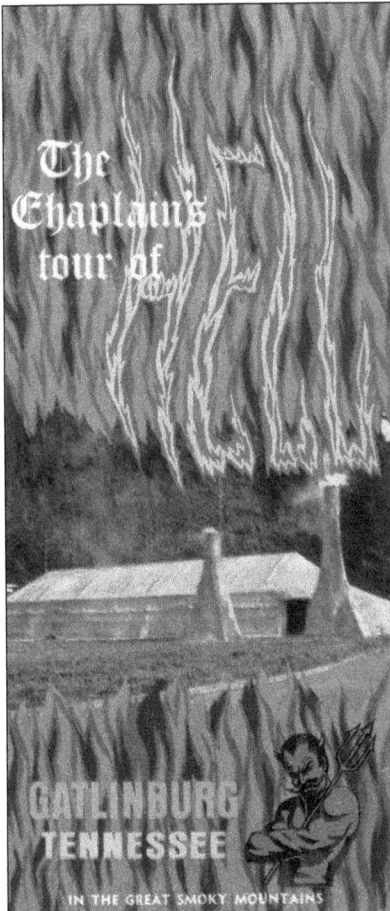

The Chaplain's "Tour Of Hell"

THE REV. MR. BUD SPRIGGS
"Chaplain of Hell"

We are in hopes this attraction will be most interesting and fascinating as well as educational and instructive.

In charge of "Hell" is a Baptist Minister, the Rev. Mr. Bud Spriggs. He will manage the exhibit here and commute back and forth to Hell, Michigan where he has a similar exhibit. This spring, the Chamber of Commerce of Hell, Michigan will officially name him the "Chaplain of Hell." Rev. Spriggs first conceived the idea of "A Tour Through Hell" from one of his sermons. The red tie, red socks, red handkerchief and red Bible are the Chaplain's trademark and can either stand for the Blood of Christ or the Fire of Hell.

Those church tour groups who made up such an important part of Smokies tourism—and still do—no doubt threw a fit when they first glimpsed the brochures for Gatlinburg's new attraction, the Museum of Witchcraft and Magic, in 1972. (Tim Hollis collection)

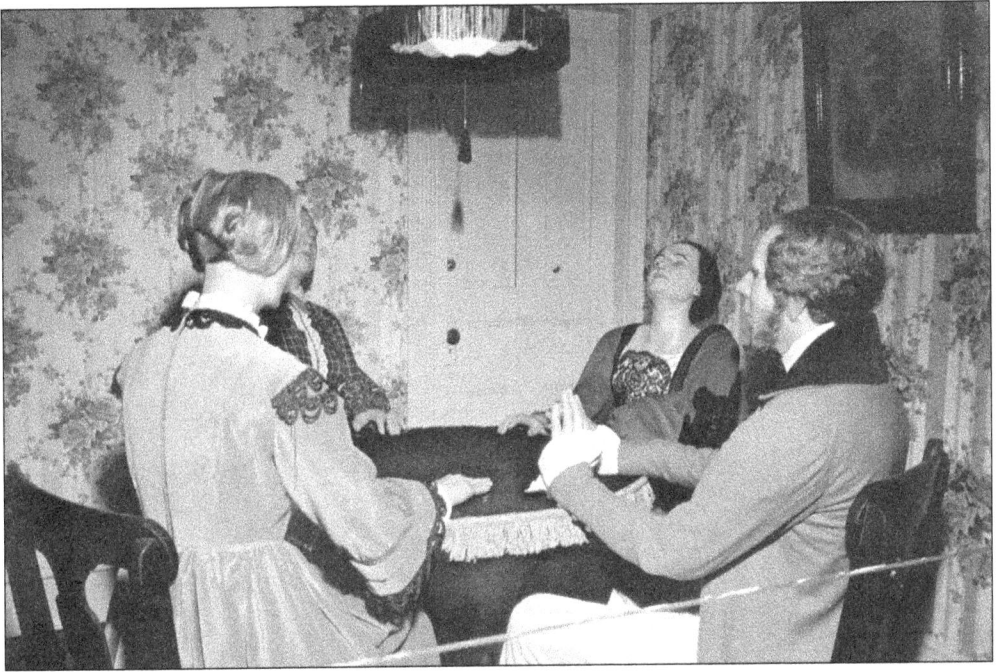

The Museum of Witchcraft and Magic was one of the Ripley organization's first Gatlinburg projects outside of the *Believe It or Not!* Museum. The wax exhibits presented any and all manner of forbidden topics, including a séance and an astrologer who looked more like Merlin the Magician. (Tim Hollis collection.)

**MEN OF THE OCCULT**
Nostradamus, the 16th cent. astrologer, predicted the two world wars, airplanes and the atom bomb. Everywhere in the museum such hauntingly life-like figures illustrate the history of the supernatural.

**WORLD'S LARGEST COLLECTION**
Visitors take a trip through the world of witchery filled with hundreds of authentic exhibits collected over 5 years in more than 75 different countries.

**BASE METALS INTO GOLD**
Cornelius Agrippa, the 15 cent. reportedly had dealings with th in one of the many carefully re

**MUSEUM OF WITCH & MA**

**THE WEREWOLF**
Is it true that Werewolves still exist in remote corners of Europe? Don't be too sure until you've seen this perfectly normal man turn into a beast — right before your eyes!

**HEAD-HUNTERS OF NEW GUINEA**
To the sound of ritual drums the Witchdoctor performs his crude dance designed to influence nature and invoke the spirits of the animal gods.

**TEST YOUR E.S.P.!**
**CAN YOU READ MINDS?**

124

**THE YOUNG WITCH**
Between 1570 and 1700, at least one million people found guilty of Witchcraft, were burned at the stake or otherwise put to death. Among the victims were thousands like the misguided young woman seen here, who is rubbing her body with "Flying Ointment".

**THE SPIRITUAL MEET**
The Spiritualist Group works together in an effort to make contact with the spirits of the dead. Listen carefully to the sounds from the 'Other World' — perhaps there is a message for you!

**BAPHOMET**
Known as the Horned God of Witches, this goat-headed Devil was the traditional figure of evil in the 1600's and is still worshipped in some Witchcraft circles today.

**BEWARE THE EVIL EYE**
Approach this person with caution. She brings on Thunder and Lightning; changes the flow of rivers; flies the skies on a broomstick — and turns her enemies into toads!

**FUN FOR ALL**
**ARE YOU A WITCH?**

If you can stand it, feast your eyes on this array of unholy inhabitants of Ripley's witchcraft museum. In the top row, you will find them using an even more taboo image than that of sorcery and devil worship: a topless woman not even attempting to conceal her breasts. Is it any wonder that the Great Smoky Mountains, one of the notches— if not the buckle— on the Bible Belt, failed to be amused by this approach to tourism? (Tim Hollis collection.)

125

FUN FOR THE WHOLE FAMILY
While in Gatlinburg Visit...

# DR. GARDNER'S

## MUSEUM OF

### MAGIC and SUPERSTITION

This unique attraction containing the world's largest collection of artifacts dealing with the Occult, was installed in Gatlinburg after 3 years of planning and research by Ripley International artists. Through the most modern and exciting methods of Sound, Light and Display, it has been acclaimed the very finest presentation of its kind in existence today.

It's Informative, Entertaining: and Fun for the Whole Family! Tel: 436-5019

Located at the junction of River Rd. and the Parkway in Gatlinburg

In a possible attempt to exorcize the reputation of the Museum of Witchcraft and Magic, in 1978 the same attraction was renamed Dr. Gardner's Museum of Magic and Superstition. The fine print in the advertisements remained the same, however, dooming the museum to the fiery pits of Bud Spriggs's concept of Hell. (Tim Hollis collection.)

Since this book began with an aerial view of some of Gatlinburg's lost attractions, it is only fitting to close it with a similar roll call for Pigeon Forge. This late-1970s shot includes (1) Magic World, (2) Smoky Mountain Car Museum, (3) Mountain Ocean, (4) Porpoise Island, (5) Hee Haw Village, and (6) a string of small motels and miniature golf courses unidentifiable from this altitude. Somehow, all of these competing businesses worked together to make the Great Smoky Mountains the tourism headquarters it is today. (Mitzi Soward collection.)

Visit us at
arcadiapublishing.com

.

www.ingramcontent.com/pod-product-compliance
Lightning Source LLC
Chambersburg PA
CBHW050650110426
42813CB00007B/1969